Vintage Texas

Cooking with Lone Star Wines

Gulf Publishing Company
Houston, Texas

Vintage Texas

Cooking with Lone Star Wines

Frank R. Giordano, Jr.

Vintage Texas
Cooking with Lone Star Wines

Gulf Publishing Company
Book Division
P.O. Box 2608 ☐ Houston, Texas 77252-2608

10   9   8   7   6   5   4   3   2   1

Library of Congress Cataloging-in-Publication Data

Giordano, Frank R., 1942–
    Vintage Texas cooking with lone star wine / Frank R. Giordano, Jr.
       p.   cm.
    Includes index.
    ISBN 0-88415-634-6
    1. Cookery (Wine)   2. Cookery–Texas.   3. Wine and wine making–Texas.   I. Title.
TX726.G53   1996
641.6'22–dc20   96-8651
                                                                        CIP

Contents

Acknowledgments

To all of you whose creations constitute this cookbook, a very grateful "Thank you." Paul and Merrill Bonarrigo of Messina Hof Wine Cellars, Ed and Susan Auler of Fall Creek Vineyards, Greg Smith and Leigh Burns of Hill Country Cellars, and Bruce Auden and Mark Bliss of Restaurant BIGA were extremely generous in supporting this work: a special "Thanks" for all of you very special people.

Several others have helped me serve up this feast of recipes. My mother—first and best of cooks—nourished my passion for foods and wine by her splendid examples in preparing and enjoying both. Margaret—second and best of cooks—has satisfied my heart and belly for more than three decades, since first appropriating my mother's recipes and wooden spoon. This book is lovingly dedicated to you both.

Friends and typists Jo DuBose and Roz Kennelly turned down the heat when deadline pressures put me in boiling soup with my publisher. Ann Criswell has shown her generous friendship once again in cooking up her fine "Foreword." And Claire Blondeau and Roxann Combs of Gulf Publishing Company set the table for the delights herein presented. Thank you all for your good work.

And to all our readers who sample these wonderful combinations of Texas wines and food, may you experience great enjoyment and well-being.

Foreword

Since I became Food Editor of the *Houston Chronicle* 30 years ago, I have been privileged to experience and write about what I think is the most exciting era in food and wine in Texas history. During this period, we have progressed from snide references to "Chateau Billy Bob" to glowing reviews—well-deserved—of several "world-class" wines.

My first taste of Texas wines at a gathering of winemakers and media in Dallas in the early 1970s was a revelation. Who would have thought that Texas could grow wines of even minimal sophistication? But there we were, tasting a lively Gewurztraminer, a fresh Chenin Blanc, and palatable hybrid red wines. Those provocative tastes offered the promise of good, even great wines, to come. The industry has not been without growing pains, of course, and some of the wines did not live up to their early promise. But many exceeded it.

As in all cultured societies, better wines begin to encourage better food, and vice versa, to create Texas Cuisine. Soon we were matching Fall Creek's Emerald Riesling with smoked wild turkey with blue cornmeal cornbread stuffing; Pheasant Ridge Cabernet Sauvignon with venison medallions and a dried cherry-Texas pecan sauce; and award-winning Ports with cheese, toasted pecans or dessert: Don Luis Port from Val Verde Winery, the outstanding 1980 Port from La Buena Vida, and Papa Paulo Port from Messina Hof. There's more to come.

This new book by Frank Giordano continues work he began in *Texas Wines and Wineries* (Texas Monthly Press, 1984), an account of the beginnings of a contemporary wine industry in the state. As interest in the increasingly fine Texas wines led naturally to a desire to use them in cooking and for accompanying special meals, Frank invited many of the top people in the wine and food industries to contribute recipes for matching Texas wines with their favorite dishes. This present cookbook provides a substantial offering of recipes that reveal some of the fascinating ways Texas winemakers, grape growers, chefs, distributors, restaurateurs, writers, and amateur cooks combine Texas wines and food. Enjoy them all! May these recipes both delight you and inspire the imaginative cook within you to create your own dining delights.

Here's a toast to the future—and the golden age—of Texas wines and food.

Ann Criswell
Food Editor, *Houston Chronicle*

Introduction

Mankind . . . possesses two supreme blessings. First of these is the goddess Demeter, or Earth—whichever name you choose to call her by. It was she who gave to man his nourishment of grain. But after her there came the son of Semele, who matched her present by inventing liquid wine as his gift to man. For filled with that good gift, suffering mankind forgets its grief; from it comes sleep; with it oblivion of the troubles of the day. There is no other medicine for misery.

Euripides, The Bacchae

Through the centuries of our evolution into civilized beings, the human race has benefited from innumerable divine blessings. And from the beginnings of our recorded history and arts, bread and wine have been valued and celebrated as the chief gifts of the gods. Like many people, I learned much about the worth and benefits of bread and wine at my family's kitchen table and at my church's altar, long before I ever heard of Euripides. And, when I first read about "Wine that maketh glad the heart of man" (Bible, Psalms 104), assent followed easily and naturally; the passage, in fact, seemed more like logic than poetry.

Like the vineyards on the Tuscan and Burgundian hillsides, this book's basic ideas—cooking with wine and matching wines with food—have been around nearly forever. But the vineyards in Texas, though much younger, have been the focus of most of my wine writing; and the subject of this book seemed to emerge inevitably once I finished *Texas Wines and Wineries* (Texas Monthly Press, 1984).

In one sense, the roots of this book are nearly as deep as I am old. I grew up in an Italian-American family in Connecticut about a half century ago, where the wine appeared as predictably as the spaghetti, the meatballs and sausage, the grated cheese and tomato sauce, and the hard-crusted bread. Life was pretty simple then: our families worked hard; ate Mom's and our aunts' hearty, nourishing meals; listened to the music of Verdi, Puccini,

Toscanini, Caruso, and Lanza; rooted for DiMaggio and Furillo and Marchiano; and drank the wines of Ernest and Julio Gallo. Life was simpler then, and life was good!

Both sets of my grandparents brought their native customs to America when they emigrated from Italy near the start of this century. Taking wine with meals suited them as well in Connecticut, where the water quality was certifiably fine, as it had in the old country. Could there be anything more natural, more normal, more satisfying than enjoying a glass of wine with a meal?

And healthy, too! While my family was growing up, my patents relied on various concoctions containing wine and whiskey to treat our minor ills and ailments. Instead of over-the-counter medications, we relied on under-the-counter jugs to restore our vigor. No less an authority than the apostle Paul advocated my parents' prescriptions: "Drink no longer water, but use a little wine for thy stomach's sake" (Bible First Epistle to Timothy).

Could a meal *be* a meal if there were no wine? Like Housman's innocent Shropshire lad, when I was one-and-twenty I instinctively knew the answers. But when I was two-and-twenty I moved to the South where many of the good country people believed that wine was brewed by the devil for the creation (or was it the destruction?) of winos. Ah, 'tis true, 'tis true!

Given the failures of Moses, Matthew, Mark, and Milton, who was I to try to explain God's ways to the southern brethren? So I left them to their malt, and I kept on sipping, knowing I could never entirely dispel their puzzling views. Meanwhile, I began writing articles on the wonderful wines of California, New York, Arkansas, and Texas. My early work on Texas culminated in *Texas Wines and Wineries,* the first book published on the state's recently reborn industry.

This current book, however, lay dormant through the first half of my twoscore years and ten, as I pruned and harvested works about literature, travel, golf—more of the gifts the gods bestow on us mortals. Then, on a business trip to San Francisco, I took a brief tour to the Napa Valley, where my professional life changed. With the first steps inside the Christian Brothers winery in St. Helena, with the first glimpse of the wooden barrels, and with the first sniff of the cool, moist, wine-drenched air, I experienced the sensual clarity and emotional force of what the poet Wordsworth called a "spot of time." In that rich moment, I was transported back to my boyhood and my maternal grandfather's cellar, a place where, unknown to me at the time, my own roots and destiny were beginning to form.

My parents' first son and the Pavones' oldest grandchild, I was occasionally privileged to join the family men after a meal, down in the cool, dank cellar. Sitting among the carpentry tools and wine barrels, where the season's freshly crushed grapes were fermenting, listening to the inscrutable Italian conversation, inhaling the scents of stogies and saw-dust, and watching the animated faces and hands amid the curling smoke, I knew, every *second* of the time, in a deeper way than consciousness, that *every* second of that time was precious. Amid the fertile pleasures of that cellar was where this book was rooted.

There have been other moments, too, when the goodness, wisdom and beauty of taking wine with meals have shown forth as in a visionary gleam. In a garden at Rambouillet outside Paris in the spring of 1978, my wife was fixing a picnic platter for our three children as we read while waiting for a tour of the ancient palace. Our limited travel budget forced her, for about the tenth day in a row, to serve the same ordinary fare at lunchtime. But Margaret was relieved when she heard our oldest son comment, "You know, Dad, this is pretty good livin'!" At the wise old age of 8, Greg knew that the Camembert cheese, the Bordeaux wine, the steaming bread fresh from the oven, and the cold ratatouille were about the best foods the plan-et had to offer. *In vino veritas,* my son. Good livin', indeed! Edward FitzGerald *(The Rubaiyat of Omar Khayyam)* could have been writing about us that splendid day.

A Book of Verses underneath the Bough,
A Jug of Wine, a Loaf of Bread—and Thou
Beside me singing in the Wilderness—
Oh, Wilderness were Paradise enow!

A day or so later, nearly exhausted from climbing and exploring Mont St. Michel, the kids mutinied and insisted we let them eat, right now, right there, at the restaurant before us. I raised Chris (age 4) and Susan (age 6), the most vocal of the pirates, and asked them to look into the restaurant widow. Greg's hunger gave way to wonder when he started describing the tables inside, with *four* wineglasses beside each plate. "That's why we're not stopping to eat here," they were told. But ever since, all three have known that an essential feature of every special meal includes wine, often several different wines.

Moments far less luminous, but equally compelling in affirming wine's centrality in a meal, occurred in obvious places like the Napa and Sonoma valleys. Joe and Alice Heitz invited my wife and me into their home when I interviewed him about his winery early in the 1980s. After finishing our work, Joe went into his garden to do some harvesting. Supper that evening would include a couple of ears of fresh corn, seasoned with butter and pepper, and a bottle of his Chardonnay. A simple meal, though fit for kings and queens.

On another occasion, Sylvia Sebastiani, in a moment of sweet candor, described how her late husband, August, delighted in outfoxing wine snobs by asking them to blindfold themselves before tasting wines. Sometimes, she chuckled, the frauds didn't even know if the wine they were tasting was white or red! She confided that August, and avid hunter and fisherman, drank Zinfandel with everything, even the bass he hooked from his favorite lake. Amen, August. Let the wine snobs pity your taste; *de gustibus* is all Greek to them anyway. A far greater pity would be a meal of freshly caught fish without wine.

The actual budding of the desire to compile a book such as the present one came while I was researching and writing about wine in the early 1980s. Whenever family or friends would gather at our home for meals, Margaret and I would often ask ourselves, "What would the winemakers serve with this meal, these dishes? How would they marry the flavors in the bottles with the flavors on the plates?" Those questions eventually fermented into this book.

The yeast that turned those questions into a cookbook, however, was the idea that wine was chiefly an alcoholic beverage. That jarring sentiment arose often in conversations with Texans. The state's laws institutionalized the idea and impeded the wine industry's growth with neo-prohibitionist regulations. It seemed to me that wine's advocates, both professional producers and lay consumers, had to educate the public and its leaders by insistently affirming that wine is a food and is consumed as part of a meal; wine is a mealtime beverage, chiefly. As Shakespeare wisely wrote, "Good wine is a good familiar creature if it be well used" (*Othello*).

I could support that educational effort, though not with rhetoric or special pleadings. Rather, with the recipes of my contributors—many of the state's top winemakers, their families and staffs; chefs in several of Texas' finest restaurants, clubs and resorts; wine distributors and retailers; wine and food writers; and enthusiastic amateur cooks. This book offers some delicious statements about wine's centrality in both the preparation and consumption of meals.

Con pan y vino se anda el camino.
(With bread and wine you can walk your road.)

Anonymous, Spanish Proverb

Appetizers
and
Soups

Baked Chevre

Serves 4–6

1	10–12 OUNCE LOG CHEVRE
¼	CUP OLIVE OIL
½	CUP FRESH BREAD CRUMBS, TOASTED

Preheat oven to 400°. Slice the cheese into ½-inch-thick rounds. Dip the rounds into the olive oil and dredge in the bread crumbs, making sure to coat them completely and evenly. Place rounds on a baking sheet and bake for 5–7 minutes, or until the cheese just begins to melt and the bottom crust is golden brown. Turn the cheese rounds brown-side up and serve hot.

Courtesy of Leigh Burns, Tasting Room Manager, Hill Country Cellars. Serve with Hill Country Cellars Johannisberg Riesling.

Chipotle Tuna Burgers with Ginger Slaw

4	OUNCES YELLOWFIN TUNA (SEE NOTE)	Serves 4
1	CHIPOTLE PEPPER, CHOPPED FINE	
1	PINCH GROUND BLACK PEPPER	
1	PINCH KOSHER SALT	
3	OUNCES SHREDDED CABBAGE	
1	OUNCE PICKLED GINGER ROOT, WITH JUICE, MINCED	
1	TEASPOON BLACK SESAME SEEDS, TOASTED	
1	TEASPOON SUGAR	
1	TABLESPOON SESAME OIL	
2	EACH SCALLIONS, SLICED THIN	
1	SMALL RED BELL PEPPER, JULIENNED FINE	
8	SLICES OF YOUR FAVORITE BREAD	
4	TEASPOONS GUACAMOLE, YOUR FAVORITE VERSION	

Combine tuna, Chipotle, ground pepper, and salt into mini-burgers. Combine cabbage, ginger, sesame seeds, sugar, oil, scallions, and bell pepper to make a slaw.

Cook burgers in a non-stick pan to brown each side, but allow center to remain rare.

Place burger on one slice of bread and top with slaw, guacamole, and second slice of bread.

Courtesy of Mark Bliss and Bruce Auden, Restaurant BIGA, San Antonio.
Notes: Use top grade tuna, center cut, chopped.
Serve with Bell Mountain Pinot Noir.

Crab or Shrimp Gumbo

Serves 4

2	STRIPS BACON
2	CUPS DICED OKRA
½	CUP DICED ONIONS
2	CUPS TOMATOES, SQUASHED
1	10¾-OUNCE CAN TOMATO SAUCE
½	LEMON, SLICED
1	BAY LEAF
1	TEASPOON RED HOT SAUCE
½	TABLESPOON BLACK PEPPER
1	TABLESPOON GUMBO FILÉ
3	CUPS WATER
3	CUPS MESSINA HOF SAUVIGNON BLANC
3	POUNDS LUMP CRAB MEAT OR
	SHELLED AND DEVEINED SHRIMP

Fry diced okra and diced onions with bacon. Add remainder of ingredients, except wine and shrimp. Simmer all ingredients about 2 hours, then add Sauvignon Blanc. Cook until the okra does not show up. Thicken with a little flour and water, then add crab meat or raw, shelled shrimp.

*Courtesy of Merrill Bonarrigo, co-owner, Messina Hof Wine Cellars.
Serve with Messina Hof Chenin Blanc.*

Curried Chicken Soup

I fondly remember a lunch on the Mosel, back in 1970. The wine: a 1966 Ürziger Würzgarten Spätlese, Mönchhof. The soup: Curried Chicken. What a revelation! It worked beautifully. Since then, I have served this combination often. To save time (and in emergencies), use canned cream of chicken soup as a base.

Serves 2

1	TABLESPOON BUTTER
1	TEASPOON CURRY POWDER
1	TABLESPOON FINELY CHOPPED ONION
½	TEASPOON CRUSHED DRIED THYME
1	10¾-OUNCE CAN OF CREAM OF CHICKEN SOUP
1	10¾-OUNCE CAN OF EVAPORATED MILK
	FRESH CARROTS AND JICAMA

Melt butter in saucepan. Add curry powder; sauté over low heat for a few seconds. Stir to blend. Add finely chopped onion and crushed thyme; sauté for about a minute. Remove from heat and let cool a few seconds. Add cream of chicken soup. A bit at a time, blend in canned milk. Stir well. Return to medium heat; cook until hot but do not boil. Serve with strips of fresh carrots and jicama.

Courtesy of Shirley Jones, Southwest editor, American Wine on the Web, *an Internet magazine.*
Serve with Messina Hof Johannisberg Riesling or Hill Country Cellars Johannisberg Riesling.

Escargots Southwest

Serves 1

1	TABLESPOON CLARIFIED BUTTER
6	ESCARGOTS
½	TEASPOON MINCED GARLIC
1 ½	OUNCES MESSINA HOF CHARDONNAY
1 ½	OUNCES FISH STOCK
1	TEASPOON SCALLIONS
1	TEASPOON LIME JUICE
1	TABLESPOON WHOLE BUTTER
1	BLUE CORN TORTILLA
	A SPRIG OF CILANTRO

Sauté escargots in clarified butter with garlic just enough to brown the garlic. Use medium heat. Deglaze with Chardonnay and fish stock. Add scallions, and finish with lime and butter. Serve on blue corn tortilla and garnish with chopped cilantro.

Courtesy of Messina Hof Wine Cellars.

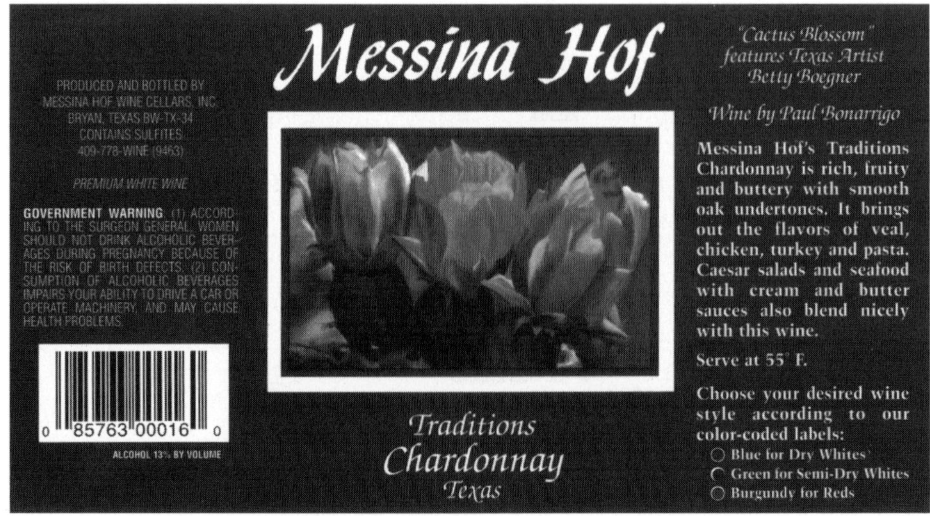

The Grape's Famous Mushroom Soup

		Serves 4–6

6   TABLESPOONS BUTTER

1   MEDIUM ONION, FINELY CHOPPED

1   POUND FRESH MUSHROOMS, RANDOMLY CHOPPED

3   TABLESPOONS FLOUR

4   CUPS BEEF BOUILLON OR BEEF STOCK

   PINCH OF WHITE PEPPER

   PINCH OF NUTMEG

1½   CUPS HEAVY CREAM

Melt butter in large saucepan. Add onion and stir over moderate heat until onion is clear. Add mushrooms and cook another 5 minutes, stirring occasionally. Blend in the flour until mixture is well-coated. Add the stock slowly, stirring continually. Bring mixture to a boil. Reduce heat and simmer 5 minutes. Add white pepper and nutmeg. Remove from heat and stir in cream.

*Courtesy of Mark Gilsdorf, The Grape Restaurant, Dallas.
Serve with Fall Creek Vineyards Chardonnay.*

Grilled Shrimp Ceviche with Riesling and Tomatillo

Serves 2–4

MESQUITE OR HICKORY WOOD FOR GRILLING

3   JUMBO SHRIMP, PEELED AND DEVEINED

7   OUNCES DRUM OR REDFISH FILLET, SKINNED AND
    DEBONED

1   TABLESPOON OLIVE OIL, EXTRA VIRGIN

1   MEDIUM ONION, FINELY DICED (DIVIDED USE)

3   SERRANO PEPPERS, FINELY DICED

1   LARGE RIPE RED TOMATO, CHOPPED

    JUICE OF 1½ LEMONS, FRESHLY SQUEEZED (DIVIDED USE)

½   CUP FALL CREEK VINEYARDS JOHANNISBERG RIESLING

1   TABLESPOON HORSERADISH

⅓   CUP KETCHUP

2   TOMATILLOS, HUSKED AND FINELY DICED

    SEA SALT (SALT CAN BE SUBSTITUTED), TO TASTE

Prepare fire, letting wood burn down to white-hot ashes. Grill shrimp and fish fillet one minute on each side to get some wood flavor. Remove from grill, cool in refrigerator.

In medium sauté pan, combine olive oil, half the chopped onion, serranos, and red tomato. Sauté 3 minutes over medium heat. Deglaze with one-eighth cup lemon juice and the Riesling, and continue to cook until mixture boils. Transfer mixture to blender, add horseradish, and purée until smooth. Pour puréed mixture into non-metal bowl and stir in ketchup, tomatillos, and remaining onion. Cool. Cover and refrigerate.

Dice chilled shrimp and fish, put in non-metal container, and pour remaining lemon juice over seafood. Cover and marinate 3 hours in refrigerator. Combine seafood and sauce, season with sea salt, and toss ingredients together lightly.

❧ *Courtesy of David Garrido, Jeffrey's Restaurant, Austin, who often teaches cooking classes at Fall Creek Vineyards.*
Serve with Fall Creek Vineyards Johannisberg Riesling.

Grilled Shrimp on Fresh Corn Cakes with Sage Butter Sauce

Corn Cakes

¼	CUP DICED RED ONION
½	CUP MINCED GREEN ONIONS
¼	CUP DICED RED BELL PEPPER
2	EARS FRESH CORN OFF THE COB
2	TABLESPOONS OLIVE OIL
3	OUNCES MESSINA HOF CHARDONNAY
4	LARGE EGGS
1	CUP MILK
2	TABLESPOONS HONEY
½	CUP FLOUR
½	CUP MASA
½	CUP CORN MEAL
	SALT AND FRESHLY GROUND BLACK PEPPER, TO TASTE

Serves 4 as appetizer, or 2 as dinner

Sauté onions, red pepper, and corn in olive oil until soft. Add wine and cook over high heat to evaporate. Set aside to cool.

Beat eggs, milk, honey, and remaining dry ingredients until smooth. Add the cooked vegetables. Adjust the seasoning with salt and pepper.

Sauté about two tablespoons of the corn cake batter in olive oil until golden brown on both sides.

Sage Butter Sauce

½   CUP MESSINA HOF CHARDONNAY

JUICE OF 1 LEMON

1   CUP HEAVY CREAM

½   CUP BUTTER, CUBED

⅓   CUP CHOPPED FRESH SAGE LEAVES

In a small saucepan, blend wine, lemon juice, and cream. Reduce by half. Whisk in butter until smooth. Add fresh chopped sage.

Grilled Shrimp

24   FRESH DEVEINED SHRIMP

LEMON PEPPER, TO TASTE

2   TABLESPOONS OLIVE OIL

Season shrimp lightly with lemon pepper. Toss in olive oil and grill. Place one shrimp on each fresh corn cake and serve with Sage Butter Sauce.

Courtesy of Jimmy Mitchell, Executive Chef, Rainbow Lodge, Houston. Serve with Messina Hof Chardonnay.

Lentil Soup

"On June 18, 1960, at 4:00 PM on pier 39 I arrived by ship as a young immigrant in New York. As I checked in at the Atlantic Sheraton Hotel I noticed a small white envelope my mother gave me at my departure in Bremerhaven. The envelope contained a few recipes and a few kind words. 'My son, very little can I give you on your long journey to America, but please accept a few of my recipes. You are a good cook; now go to America and make a new life for yourself.'"
—Joe Mannke, owner and chef, Rotisserie for Beef and Bird, Houston.

In this same spirit of generosity, Joe Mannke has offered some of his and his mother's recipes—gifts that have guided him to a very successful career in the New World over the last 35 years—for this book. Thank you, both of you.—The Author

1	POUND LENTILS	Serves 8
¼	STICK OF BUTTER	
2	SLICES BACON, FINELY CHOPPED	
½	CUP ONIONS, DICED	
½	CUP CELERY, DICED	
2	CLOVES GARLIC CHOPPED	
1	TABLESPOON FLOUR	
1	SMOKED PIG KNUCKLE (OPTIONAL)	
½	CUP CARROTS, DICED	
2	QUARTS (8 CUPS) BEEF STOCK	
8	OUNCES SMOKED SAUSAGE, SLICED	
½	TEASPOON SALT	
	DASH OF BLACK PEPPER	
1	TEASPOON FRENCH MUSTARD	

Soak the lentils in 10 cups water for 10 hours, then drain.

Melt the butter in a Dutch oven, add the chopped bacon, onion, celery, and garlic. Simmer over low heat until tender. Combine with the flour, add the lentils, pig knuckle, and beef broth. Bring to a boil, then reduce heat. Simmer for two hours, stirring occasionally.

Add sliced smoked sausage, salt, pepper, one teaspoon French mustard and serve in warmed bowls.

❧ Serve with Bell Mountain Pinot Noir.

Medallion of Fresh Tuna Wrapped in Bacon and Served with a Merlot Sauce

Serves 1

1   3½-OUNCE FRESH TUNA MEDALLION

1   THICK SLICE BACON

Cook the bacon just until it is limp, but still loose enough to wrap the medallion. Cut the tuna (about 2½ inches in height and 2 inches in diameter) and wrap with bacon, holding it in place with a toothpick. Grill about 2 minutes on each side, then turn on side to cook bacon. Serve medium rare on bed of Red Wine Sauce (recipe follows) with a vegetable relish.

Red Wine Sauce for Tuna

Serves 4

2   SHALLOTS, THIN SLICED

8   OUNCES PHEASANT RIDGE MERLOT

4   OUNCES UNSALTED BUTTER

   SALT AND BLACK PEPPER, TO TASTE

Reduce shallots and red wine by ¾ at low simmer, so as not to bruise wine. Rapidly whisk in butter, add salt and pepper to taste, and strain.

❧ Courtesy of David Schnell, Executive Chef, Houston Club.
Serve with Messina Hof Gamay Beaujolais.

Molasses Grilled Texas Quail in a Fried Sweet Onion Cup with Tomatillo Jalapeño Chutney

For more than a decade, the Houston Club has conducted the Best of Texas Wine Awards and Tasting, two events that celebrate the finest wines produced in the state. This appetizer was prepared by Executive Chef David Schnell for a Retrospective Dinner, featuring the Best of Texas medal winners from 1994, on September 14, 1995, at the Houston Club.

Serves 8

8	PARTIALLY BONED QUAIL
16	OUNCES TOMATILLO JALAPEÑO CHUTNEY (RECIPE FOLLOWS)
8	HALVES TEXAS SWEET ONIONS
	BUTTERMILK, AS NEEDED
	SPRIG OF FRESH THYME
	ALL-PURPOSE FLOUR, AS NEEDED
	SALT AND PEPPER, AS NEEDED

Hollow out onions to form onion cups. Cover the onion cups with buttermilk and refrigerate for 2 hours. Season the flour with salt and pepper.

Place the quail on the grill, breast side down, for 3 minutes; then turn over for another 2 minutes. While quail is cooking, dredge onion cups in seasoned flour, and deep fry to golden brown. Drain well.

Molasses Marinade

½   CUP SOY SAUCE

¼   CUP SHINER BOCK BEER

2   TABLESPOONS MOLASSES

    ZEST OF ONE ORANGE

    ZEST OF ONE LEMON

1   TABLESPOON CHOPPED FRESH THYME

2   TEASPOONS FRESH LEMON JUICE

4   TABLESPOONS PEELED, DICED GINGER

2   TEASPOONS MINCED GARLIC

For the marinade, place all ingredients into a bowl and mix well. Place quail into marinade and refrigerate for 4 hours. Remove quail and drain.

Tomatillo Jalapeño Chutney

1   POUND DICED TOMATILLO, HUSK REMOVED

1   CUP FINELY DICED RED ONIONS

½   CUP FINELY DICED GREEN BELL PEPPER

6   SEEDED AND MINCED JALAPEÑOS

8   THINLY SLICED GREEN ONIONS

½   CUP FRESH CORN KERNELS

¼   CUP BROWN SUGAR

2   TABLESPOONS FINELY DICED CILANTRO

1   TEASPOON MINCED GARLIC

½   TEASPOON CUMIN POWDER

Place all ingredients into saucepan and simmer for 30 minutes until thickened.

To serve, place onion cup in center of plate and ladle chutney around. Cut the quail in half down the breast and crisscross in onion cup. Garnish with a sprig of fresh thyme

❧ Courtesy of David Schnell, Executive Chef, The Houston Club. Serve with Ste. Genevieve Proprietor's Reserve Chardonnay.

Potato Cheese Soup

Serves 4 or 5

3	MEDIUM POTATOES
1	SMALL ONION, FINELY CHOPPED (¼ CUP)
½	CUP BOILING, LIGHTLY SALTED WATER
½	CUP MESSINA HOF CHENIN BLANC
	MILK
2	TABLESPOONS BUTTER, MELTED
2	TABLESPOONS ALL-PURPOSE FLOUR
2	TABLESPOONS SNIPPED PARSLEY
¾	TEASPOON SALT
	FRESHLY GROUND PEPPER
1	CUP SHREDDED NATURAL SWISS CHEESE (OR JALAPEÑO CHEDDAR FOR SPICIER SOUP)

Wash and pare potatoes; cut up. In 2-quart saucepan, add potatoes and onion to the boiling water. Add wine. Cover and cook until potatoes are tender, about 20 minutes. Mash slightly; do not drain. Measure mixture and add enough milk to make 5 cups. Blend melted butter, flour, parsley, salt, and pepper. Stir into potato mixture in saucepan; cook and stir until mixture thickens and bubbles. Add cheese; cook and stir until cheese is partially melted. Garnish with parsley and serve immediately.

❧ Courtesy of Messina Hof Wine Cellars.

Sage-roasted Quail with Herbed Potato Pancakes

"These go well with roasted vegetables for a main meal, or top the potato pancakes with a mescalun mix for a fabulous first course. I especially like to serve a creamy soy-shiitake vinaigrette as an accompaniment."—Melody Wolfertz, Executive Chef—Marty's, Merchants of Fine Foods & Wine, Dallas.

Quail

8 appetizer or 4 entree portions

8	SEMI-BONELESS QUAIL, PATTED DRY
8	FRESH SAGE LEAVES
8	TABLESPOONS OLIVE OIL
1 TO 2	SHALLOTS, MINCED
1	TEASPOON FRESH THYME, CHOPPED
1	TEASPOON CRACKED BLACK PEPPER
1	TEASPOON KOSHER SALT

Stuff a sage leaf into the cavity of each quail.

Combine oil, shallots, and seasonings; pour over quail, and rub to coat. Refrigerate and allow to marinate overnight.

Remove quail from oil and grill or sauté to medium or medium-rare.

❧ *Note: Overcooked quail tend to taste like liver, so definitely enjoy these birds while they are pink.*

Potato Pancakes

6 MEDIUM YUKON GOLD POTATOES, GRATED AND
  SQUEEZED TO REMOVE WATER

1 SMALL ONION, GRATED

1 TEASPOON FRESH SAGE

1 TEASPOON FRESH THYME

1 LARGE EGG

1 TEASPOON FRESH GROUND PEPPER

1 TEASPOON KOSHER SALT

 BUTTER AND OLIVE OIL TO SAUTÉ

Combine all ingredients except butter and oil. Test seasonings and adjust to taste. Heat oil and butter in pan to sizzling, drop small mounds of batter into pan, and flatten gently. Sauté until golden and crispy. Keep warm until ready to serve.

❧ *Serve with Ste. Genevieve Merlot.*

Sea Scallops a la Plancha on Clam Texmati Paella

"A la Plancha: This is a technique that I learned while traveling through Spain. A heavy iron griddle is heated until hot and then various simply seasoned meats, fish, and vegetables are seared very quickly and served drizzled with olive oil and lemon."—Mark Bliss, Chef de Cuisine, Restaurant BIGA, San Antonio

Serves 6

6	JUMBO SEA SCALLOPS
18	MANILA OR OTHER SMALL CLAMS
	KOSHER SALT AND PEPPER
3	CUPS CHICKEN STOCK
1	PINCH SAFFRON
2	TABLESPOONS PURE OLIVE OIL
2	CLOVES MINCED GARLIC
½	MEDIUM DICED ONION
1	RED ANAHEIM CHILE PEPPER, DE-RIBBED, PEELED, SEEDED, AND DICED
1½	CUPS TEXMATI RICE
½	CUP FRESH PEAS
1	TABLESPOON SPANISH SHERRY VINEGAR
2	OUNCES GARLIC OIL (RECIPE FOLLOWS)
2	OUNCES BASIL OIL

Scallops

Try to find dry-pack or day-boat scallops. These giants are packed without any preservatives and have a much better flavor than those packed in liquid. If you cannot find them, try to find fresh sea scallops. In either case, you will need to remove the side "band" that the scallop uses to attach itself to the shell. Place in the refrigerator and reserve.

Clams

At Restaurant BIGA, I try to use Manila clams when available. They have a very tender sweet meat that is absolutely delicious. A good substitute would be littleneck clams. Since clams tend to be sandy, you must scrub them under running water to remove any grit.

Roast Tomato and Garlic Vinaigrette

8   ROMA TOMATOES, RIPE

1   SHALLOT

1   OUNCE SHERRY VINEGAR

2   OUNCES GARLIC OIL (RECIPE FOLLOWS)

4   CLOVES ROASTED GARLIC (RECIPE FOLLOWS)

    SALT AND PEPPER

    BASIL SPRIGS

Place tomatoes on sheet pan in 400° oven and roast until slightly charred, 30–40 minutes. Place tomatoes, shallot, vinegar, oil, and garlic in blender and purée. Strain through chinois (fine mesh strainer), and season with salt and pepper. Steep basil in sauce. Set aside and keep warm.

❧ *Can substitute canned plum tomatoes.*

Roast Garlic Oil

24   CLOVES GARLIC

2   CUPS OLIVE OIL (NOT EXTRA VIRGIN)

Place garlic in oil over medium heat and "roast" approximately 25–30 minutes. Strain. Use oil and cloves separately in above recipe.

Saffron Broth

Heat 3 cups homemade or good quality chicken stock over medium high heat and stir in saffron. Keep this warm.

Basil Oil

1   CUP FRESH BASIL, LEAVES ONLY
2   QUARTS BOILING HOT WATER
1   CUP EXTRA VIRGIN OLIVE OIL

Blanch basil in boiling water for 15–20 seconds. Refresh in ice bath, drain, and dry well. Place basil in blender with extra virgin olive oil and blend one minute. Strain through a paper coffee filter. Basil oil will keep refrigerated in a tightly sealed container for one week.

Rice

Set a 4 quart, 2½″ deep skillet over medium heat. Add olive oil, stir in diced onion, and sauté until translucent, 5–6 minutes. Add the diced Anaheim chile pepper and garlic, and cook for 1–2 minutes. Stir in the rice and sauté until rice begins to turn white. Add the warm saffron broth, stirring to mix the ingredients. Taste broth and add salt and pepper if necessary. Cover and bring to a boil. Reduce heat to a simmer. When the broth has reduced to the level of the rice (about 5–7 minutes), place the clams around the edge of the skillet and scatter the peas over the top and cover. Cook another 15 minutes until rice is done. Remove from heat and keep warm until ready to serve.

✿ *Serve with Fall Creek Vineyards Sauvignon Blanc.*

Texas 1015 Wine Soup

¼	CUP BUTTER OR MARGARINE	Serves 6–8
5	LARGE TEXAS 1015 ONIONS, CHOPPED	
5	CUPS BROTH OR BOUILLON	
½	CUP CELERY LEAVES	
1	LARGE POTATO	
1	CUP CAP*ROCK CHARDONNAY	
1	TABLESPOON VINEGAR	
2	TEASPOONS SUGAR	
1	CUP LIGHT CREAM	
1	TABLESPOON MINCED PARSLEY	
	SALT AND PEPPER, TO TASTE	

Heat butter in large saucepan; add onion and cook 5 minutes. Add broth, celery leaves, and potato; bring to a boil, simmer, and cover 30 minutes. Sieve mixture or purée. Return mixture to saucepan. Blend in wine, vinegar, and sugar. Bring to a boil, reduce heat, and simmer 5 minutes. Stir in cream, parsley, and salt and pepper to taste. Heat thoroughly; stir often; do not boil.

Courtesy of Mary Burge, wife of Stu Burge, Executive Director, Texas Grape Growers Association, Colleyville.

Fish and Seafood

Broiled Bass with Anisette Pepper Sauce

Serves 6

6   FILLETS OF BASS OR ANY WHITE FISH, ABOUT 8 OUNCES
    EACH

3   MEDIUM RED BELL PEPPERS, JULIENNED

2   TABLESPOONS BUTTER

¼   CUP ANISETTE

1   CUP HEAVY CREAM

¼   CUP TOMATO SAUCE

¼   CUP ANISE NEEDLES OR CHOPPED PARSLEY

    SALT AND PEPPER

Preheat broiler. Place fish on broiling pan and sprinkle lightly with water to prevent sticking. Broil about 6" from heat source, 5–10 minutes or until fish becomes pearly white and flakes when tested with a fork. While fish broils, prepare sauce by sautéing peppers until they become limp. Add anisette, heavy cream, and tomato sauce; cook until reduced by half. Mix in anise needles. Season with salt and pepper to taste.

Courtesy of John Rydman, Spec's Liquor Stores, Houston.
Serve with Messina Hof Pinot Noir.

Crab Cakes
with Red Chili Caper Aioli
and Thai Vegetable Slaw

Crab Cakes

Serves 4–6

1	POUND BLUE CRAB MEAT, CLEANED
1	SMALL RED ONION, FINELY CHOPPED
¼	CUP FINELY CHOPPED GREEN ONIONS
1	CLOVE GARLIC, MINCED
1	SMALL RED PEPPER, SEEDED AND DICED
½	CUP MAYONNAISE
1	TABLESPOON DIJON MUSTARD
¼	CUP SMALL CAPERS
1	CUP WHITE BREAD CRUMBS
1	TABLESPOON FLOUR, PLUS EXTRA FOR BREADING
1	DASH EACH TABASCO, WORCESTERSHIRE SAUCE, SALT, AND WHITE PEPPER
6	TABLESPOONS BUTTER

Combine all ingredients except butter in mixing bowl. Form into about 8 cakes, each ½-inch thick. Lightly flour and pan fry in butter until golden brown on both sides. Spoon Red Chili Caper Aioli on serving plates and top with crab cakes. Garnish with crisp greens, Thai Vegetable Slaw, and lemon wedges.

Red Chili Caper Aioli

4	EGG YOLKS
2	CUPS OLIVE OIL
1	CLOVE GARLIC, MINCED
1	TABLESPOON RICE WINE VINEGAR
2	TABLESPOONS RED CHILI PASTE (MADE FROM SOAKED AND PURÉED DRIED CHILIES)
¼	CUP SMALL CAPERS
1	DASH SALT AND WHITE PEPPER

Beat egg yolks with a hand-held whisk or mixer, slowly adding olive oil to make an emulsion the consistency of mayonnaise. Slowly mix in all remaining ingredients. Chill 30 minutes before serving.

Thai Vegetable Slaw

1	MEDIUM CARROT, CUT INTO MATCHSTICKS
1	ZUCCHINI, CUT INTO MATCHSTICKS
1	CUCUMBER, CUT INTO MATCHSTICKS
¼	RED CABBAGE, CUT INTO MATCHSTICKS
2	TABLESPOONS RICE WINE VINEGAR
1	DASH THAI SIRACHE OR OTHER RED PEPPER SAUCE
1	TABLESPOON SUGAR
1	DASH SALT AND WHITE PEPPER

Toss vegetables together. Combine liquids and seasonings, and toss with the slaw. Chill to crisp.

❧ *Courtesy of Mark Gilsdorf, The Grape Restaurant, Dallas.*
Serve with Fall Creek Vineyards Chardonnay.

Crawfish or Shrimp Etouffee

Seasoning

Serves 8

2   TEASPOONS SALT

2   TEASPOONS GROUND RED PEPPER, PREFERABLY
      CAYENNE

1   TEASPOON WHITE PEPPER

1   TEASPOON BLACK PEPPER

1   TEASPOON DRIED SWEET BASIL LEAVES

½   TEASPOON DRIED THYME LEAVES

Sauce

¼   CUP CHOPPED ONION

¼   CUP CHOPPED CELERY

¼   CUP CHOPPED GREEN BELL PEPPER

7   TABLESPOONS VEGETABLE OIL

¾   CUP ALL-PURPOSE FLOUR

3   CUPS BASIC SEAFOOD STOCK

½   POUND (2 STICKS) UNSALTED BUTTER

2   POUNDS PEELED CRAWFISH TAILS OR MEDIUM SHRIMP

1   CUP VERY FINELY CHOPPED GREEN ONION

4   CUPS HOT COOKED RICE

Thoroughly combine seasoning ingredients in a small bowl and set aside. In separate bowl combine onions, celery, and bell pepper.

In large heavy skillet (preferably cast iron), heat the oil on high heat until it begins to smoke, about 4 minutes. With a long-handled metal whisk, gradually mix in the flour, stirring until smooth. Continue cooking, whisking constantly, until roux is dark red-brown, about 3–5 minutes. Remove from heat and immediately stir in the vegetables and 1 tablespoon of the seasoning mix with a wooden spoon; continue stirring until cooled, about

5 minutes. In a 2-quart saucepan, bring 2 cups of the stock to a boil over high heat. Gradually add the roux and whisk until thoroughly dissolved. Reduce heat to low and cook until flour taste is gone, about 2 minutes, whisking almost constantly. Remove from heat and set aside. Heat the serving plates in a 250° oven.

In a 4-quart saucepan, melt 1 stick of butter over medium heat. Stir in the crawfish (or shrimp) and the green onions; sauté about 1 minute, stirring almost constantly. Add the remaining stick of butter, the stock mixture, and the remaining 1 cup stock; cook until butter melts and is mixed into the sauce, about 4 to 6 minutes, constantly shaking the pan in a back and forth motion. Add the remaining seasoning mix; stir well and remove from heat. (If sauce starts separating, add about 2 tablespoons stock or water and shake pan until it combines.) Serve over rice.

✤ *Courtesy of Leigh Burns, Tasting Room manager, Hill Country Cellars. Serve with Hill Country Cellars Chardonnay.*

Deviled Crab

Serves 4

¼	CUP ONION, CHOPPED VERY FINE
½	CUP CELERY, CHOPPED VERY FINE
	OLIVE OIL
¼	CUP LLANO ESTACADO SAUVIGNON BLANC
5	OUNCES CREAM OF MUSHROOM SOUP (½ CAN)
½	TEASPOON SALT
¼	TEASPOON PEPPER
½	TEASPOON GARLIC POWDER
1	TEASPOON WORCESTERSHIRE SAUCE
6 TO 8	DROPS OF HOT PEPPER SAUCE
1	CUP HEAVY CREAM
1	TABLESPOON FRESH LEMON JUICE
1 TO 1½	POUNDS CRAB MEAT
1	CUP BREAD CRUMBS

Sauté onion and celery in olive oil. Add wine, simmer five minutes. Mix soup, spices, and the rest of the ingredients. Add to sautéed mixture. Heat to just boiling, then add crab meat and bread crumbs.

Place in individual casserole dishes, and top with additional bread crumbs. Bake at 350° until bubbly throughout.

❧ *Courtesy of Mary Louise Fuchs, Llano Estacado Winery, Lubbock.*

Gaido's Fried Shrimp

Serves 4–6

1	CUP MILK
2	EGGS
2	CUPS CRACKER MEAL
	WHITE PEPPER
	SALT
2	POUNDS SHRIMP
	VEGETABLE OIL

Whip eggs and milk together. Sift cracker meal, salt, and pepper together in a large shallow pan. Soak shrimp in milk and egg batter 30–60 seconds. Remove and drain. Place shrimp in breading, patting gently with the heel of your hand so breading adheres to the surface of the shrimp. Shake gently to remove excess breading.

Heat vegetable oil to 350° in a deep pot. Submerge shrimp totally in the oil. Do not crowd too many shrimp into the pot at the same time. Fry until golden brown. Drain excess oil from shrimp by placing on a rack or screen, turning shrimp once or twice to drain as much oil as possible. Place shrimp on a paper towel and dab lightly to remove any remaining oil.

❧ *Courtesy of Jay Gazzier, Gaido's Restaurant, Galveston.*
Serve with Fall Creek Emerald Riesling.

Grilled Catfish with Avocado Mayonnaise

Catfish is a delicious delicate fish and perfect for grilling. This popular fish can be found in lakes and streams throughout Texas, and farm-fresh catfish is readily available at supermarkets everywhere.

6 CATFISH FILLETS

Serves 6

Marinade

1   TABLESPOON MINCED GARLIC

1   CUP SAFFLOWER OIL

2   TEASPOONS MINCED BASIL OR CILANTRO

Mix marinade and soak fillets for 1 hour. Remove fillets from marinade and place on hot greased grill. Grill for 4–5 minutes each side, being careful not to overcook. Salt and pepper lightly. Strain basil and garlic from oil, and cool oil in pan.

Avocado Mayonnaise

1   RIPE AVOCADO

1   TABLESPOON BALSAMIC VINEGAR

1   TABLESPOON LIME JUICE

1   TEASPOON DIJON MUSTARD

½   TEASPOON SALT

3   EGG YOLKS

   REMAINING MARINADE

Purée avocado, salt, and lime juice in blender or food processor. In saucepan, simmer basil and garlic in vinegar until almost completely evaporated. Add basil and garlic to blender with mustard and egg yolks. Blend until smooth and, with motor running, add remaining oil from marinade. Blend until creamy and thick. Then add avocado mixture to blender and blend. Keep warm in top of double boiler. Serve with grilled catfish.

*❀ Courtesy of Susan Auler, co-owner, Fall Creek Vineyards.
Serve with Fall Creek Vineyards Sauvignon Blanc or Chardonnay.*

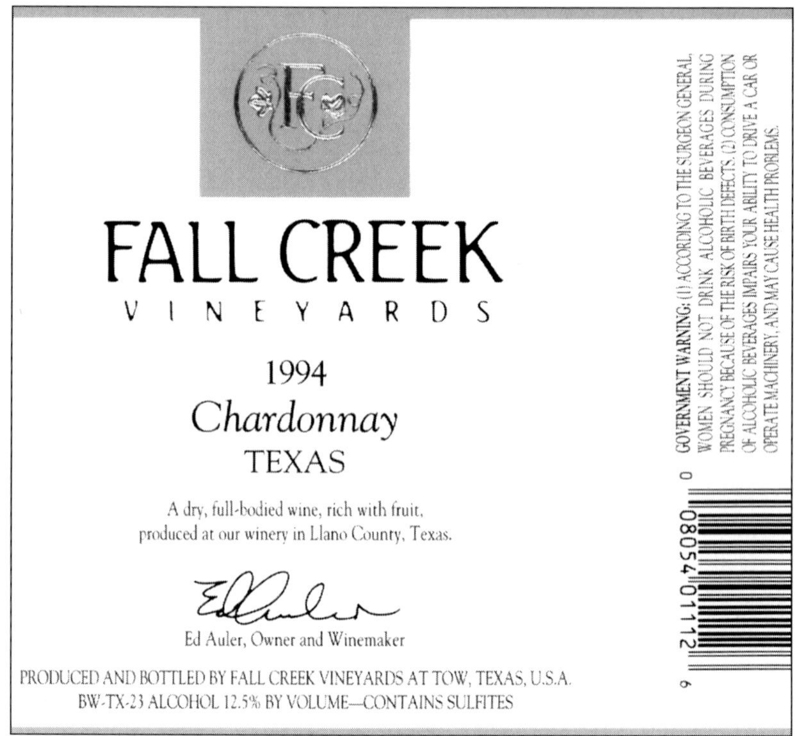

Hazelnut-crusted Seabass with Saffron and Citrus

3	POUNDS SEABASS OR OTHER FIRM-FLESHED WHITEFISH
½	CUP CHOPPED HAZELNUTS
¼	CUP FLOUR
¼	CUP HALF AND HALF
2	TABLESPOONS CHOPPED CHERVIL OR ITALIAN PARSLEY
	SALT AND PEPPER, TO TASTE
	SAFFRON LIME SAUCE (RECIPE FOLLOWS)
	ROAST GARLIC MASHED POTATOES (RECIPE FOLLOWS)
	SAUTÉED SPINACH (RECIPE FOLLOWS)
24	POMEGRANATE SEEDS
1	RUBY RED GRAPEFRUIT, SECTIONED

Seabass

Divide seabass into 6 equal portions, approximately 7.5 ounces each. Lightly season flour with salt and pepper. Dredge top of seabass with flour, then dip into half and half. Combine hazelnuts and chervil on a plate and press moistened top of seabass into mix. Refrigerate until ready to bake.

Preheat oven to 400°. Coat a cookie sheet with non-stick cooking spray and place each portion on pan. Put in oven on center rack and bake 15–17 minutes. Hazelnuts should be lightly toasted, and fish will feel firm to the touch. Keep warm until ready to serve, but don't wait longer than 10 minutes, as the fish will dry out.

Roast Garlic Mashers

Make mashed potatoes as you normally would and mix in mashed roast garlic cloves to taste.

Saffron Lime Sauce

2	CHOPPED SHALLOTS
2	CUPS LLANO ESTACADO SIGNATURE WHITE
	JUICE OF 1 LIME
1	PINCH SAFFRON
2	OUNCES HEAVY CREAM
8	OUNCES UNSALTED BUTTER, CUBED, ROOM TEMPERATURE

Place shallots in small saucepan with wine, saffron, and lime juice. Reduce until almost dry. Add heavy cream and bring to a simmer. Off the stove or over very low heat, whisk in butter until fully incorporated. Hold in a warm area until ready to use.

Sautéed Spinach

In a heavy skillet over medium heat, place 1 tablespoon butter, olive oil, and 2 cloves chopped garlic. Allow garlic to brown lightly. Add 1 pound washed, stemmed, and dried spinach. Cook over medium heat. Set aside and keep warm.

Place mashed potatoes on plate and top with spinach and seabass. Lightly cover with saffron lime sauce and garnish with pomegranate seeds and grapefruit sections. If chervil sprigs are available, place one atop each fish.

✿ *Courtesy of Mark Bliss, Chef de Cuisine, Restaurant BIGA, San Antonio. Serve with Fall Creek Vineyards Semillon-Sauvignon Blanc.*

Mesa Salmon

Serves 4

4	SALMON STEAKS
1	CUP LLANO ESTACADO CHARDONNAY
1	SMALL LIME

Put the salmon steaks in a shallow pan, squeeze the lime juice over the top of each steak, then pour the wine over the steaks and lightly season with your favorite fish seasonings. Cover and refrigerate for one hour. Remove from refrigerator, and grill for approximately 3 minutes on each side.

Fresh Fruit Salsa

1	MEDIUM CANTALOUPE
1	LEMON
2	LIMES
¼	CUP LLANO ESTACADO CHARDONNAY
2	JALAPEÑO PEPPERS
¼	CUP FRESH CILANTRO

Remove rind and seeds from cantaloupe and chop into bite-sized pieces. Set aside in a bowl. Mix with diced jalapeño peppers.

Combine the lemon and lime juice with the wine and mix well. Add cilantro and let sit for 10 minutes. Pour the juice mixture over the cantaloupe and peppers, and toss well. Refrigerate for one hour. Serve chilled salsa over the top of the grilled salmon steaks.

This recipe can be used for a variety of fish, such as shark, swordfish, and halibut. You can also make the Fruit Salsa with fresh peaches or fresh mango. If using mangoes, it is best to warm the salsa mixture slightly in the microwave before topping the grilled fish.

❧ *Courtesy of Bill Delassandro, Food Consultant for Llano Estacado Winery, Lubbock.*

Mixed Seafood Grill with Golden Tomato Salsa and Jicama-Melon Relish

Serves 4

1	RED SNAPPER FILLET, 6–8 OUNCES
1	CENTER-CUT SWORDFISH FILLET, 6–8 OUNCES
8	MEDIUM RAW SHRIMP, PEELED AND DEVEINED
	VEGETABLE OIL FOR BRUSHING
	SALT AND FRESHLY GROUND BLACK PEPPER, TO TASTE
3	CUPS GOLDEN TOMATO SALSA (RECIPE FOLLOWS)
	JICAMA-MELON RELISH (RECIPE FOLLOWS)

Preheat and lightly oil bars of grill. If using wooden skewers, soak them in water to prevent them from burning.

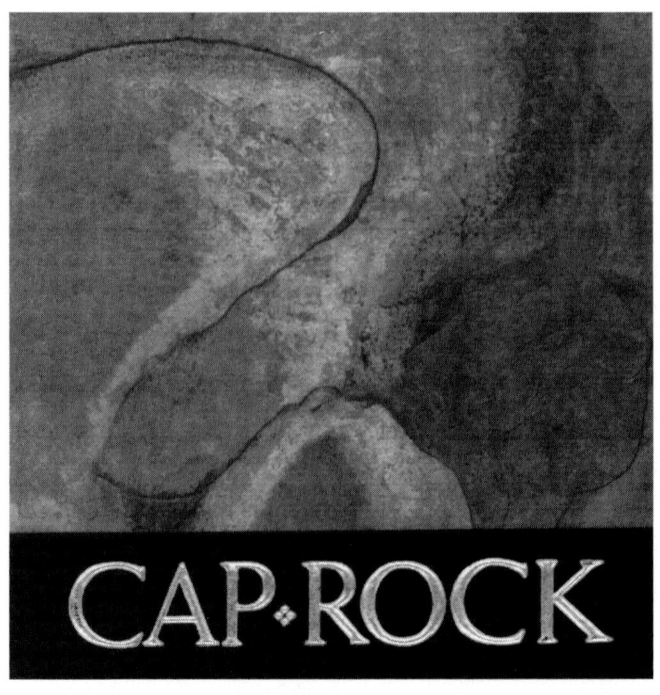

Cut the snapper and swordfish into 4 equal portions. On each of 4 skewers, place 1 shrimp, 1 portion of snapper, another shrimp, and a portion of swordfish. Brush the skewers with oil and season with salt and pepper. Place the skewers on the grill and cook for 2–3 minutes per side.

Transfer the skewers to serving plates and serve with Golden Tomato Salsa and Jicama Melon Relish.

Golden Tomato Salsa

1	POUND RIPE YELLOW TOMATOES, HALVED, SEEDED, AND DICED
2	TABLESPOONS DICED RED BELL PEPPER
2	TABLESPOONS DICED GREEN BELL PEPPER
2	TABLESPOONS DICED YELLOW BELL PEPPER
2	TABLESPOONS DICED CHIVES
2	SERRANO CHILIES, SEEDED, DERIBBED, AND MINCED
1	TABLESPOON FRUIT VINEGAR
1	TABLESPOON FRESH LIME JUICE
	SALT AND FRESHLY GROUND BLACK PEPPER, TO TASTE
1	TABLESPOON CHOPPED CILANTRO

In a mixing bowl, combine the tomatoes, bell peppers, chives, and serranos. Toss and season with the vinegar, lime juice, salt, pepper, and cilantro. Serve slightly warmed.

Jicama-Melon Relish

1	SMALL MANGO, PEELED AND PITTED
1	SERRANO CHILE, SEEDED AND DERIBBED
	JUICE OF 1 LIME
1½	TABLESPOONS RED BELL PEPPER, DICED INTO ⅛-INCH CUBES
½	CUP HONEYDEW, DICED INTO ¼-INCH CUBES
2	TABLESPOONS CUCUMBER, PEELED, SEEDED AND DICED INTO ¼-INCH CUBES
½	CUP JICAMA, PEELED AND DICED INTO ¼-INCH CUBES
2	TEASPOONS CHOPPED CILANTRO
¼	TEASPOON SALT
2	TABLESPOONS SOUR CREAM

In a food processor or blender, purée the mango with the serrano chile and lime juice. Place the diced vegetables and fruit in a mixing bowl, add the purée, and thoroughly combine. Mix in the cilantro, salt, and pepper, and adjust seasoning to taste. Gently fold in the sour cream and serve immediately.

❧ *Courtesy of Stephan Pyles, Star Canyon Restaurant, Dallas.
Serve with Cap*Rock Brut.*

Orange Butter Bass

Serves 4

2	POUNDS BASS FILLETS, SKINNED AND CUT INTO 4 EQUAL PORTIONS
	SALT AND PEPPER
2	TABLESPOONS GRATED ORANGE ZEST
2	TABLESPOONS GRATED LEMON ZEST
2	TABLESPOONS MINCED SCALLIONS (WHITE PART ONLY)
1 ½	TABLESPOONS MINCED FRESH PARSLEY
6	TABLESPOONS UNSALTED BUTTER

Preheat oven to 350°. Butter a shallow baking dish large enough to hold fish in a single layer.

Season fish on both sides: generously with salt, and lightly with pepper. Arrange in the baking dish. Sprinkle the fish with orange zest, lemon zest, scallions, and parsley. Dot with butter.

Bake for 15–18 minutes, basting twice, until fish barely separates when tested with a spoon. Serve with pan juices spooned over fish. Garnish with parsley sprigs.

❧ Courtesy of Hill Country Cellars.
Serve with Hill Country Cellars Chardonnay.

Pecan-crusted Trout with Rio Grande Citrus Beurre Blanc

Serves 2

12	OUNCES TROUT FILLETS
2	OUNCES PECANS
½	OUNCE BREAD CRUMBS
1	TABLESPOON FRESH BASIL, CHOPPED FINE
1	TABLESPOON FRESH MARJORAM, CHOPPED FINE
2	TEASPOONS FRESH LIME JUICE
	SALT, TO TASTE
	FRESH GROUND BLACK PEPPER, TO TASTE
	CAYENNE PEPPER, TO TASTE

Place pecans, bread crumbs, basil, marjoram, salt, and pepper in a food processor. Chop using the pulse feature (on and quickly off) until largest pecan pieces are ¼ inch in size. Place mixture into flat pan. Season trout with salt, pepper, and ½ lime juice. Firmly press seasoned trout into pecan mixture. Turn trout over and repeat. Be sure trout is completely covered with pecan mixture. Place trout in a non-stick baking dish and bake at 350° for 7–8 minutes or until trout is done; or sauté in a non-stick skillet with 1–2 tablespoons olive oil on medium heat until done. Place trout on plate and top with remaining lime juice.

Pour Rio Grande Citrus Beurre Blanc over one half of trout, with some extra on the plate. Garnish with sections of fresh grapefruit .

Rio Grande Citrus Beurre Blanc with Messina Hof Chardonnay

2   OUNCES SHALLOT

1   OUNCE GARLIC, CHOPPED

2   OUNCES ORANGE JUICE

2   OUNCES LIME JUICE

2   OUNCES RUBY RED GRAPEFRUIT JUICE

1   TABLESPOON SEASONED SALT, OR SALT AND PEPPER

2   OUNCES MESSINA HOF CHARDONNAY

3   OUNCES HEAVY CREAM

1   POUND BUTTER, IN SMALL PIECES

JUICE OF ½ LIME (RESERVE)

Place shallots, garlic, juice, seasoned salt, and Messina Hof Chardonnay in a pot; reduce until thick. Turn heat to very low, add cream, and then add butter, whisking constantly. Move pot on and off heat so mixture stays warm, but never hot. When all butter has been melted in, remove from heat, stir in reserved lime juice, and hold in warm place until serving.

Courtesy of Chef Charles Watkins, owner and chef, Sierra Grill, Houston. Serve with Messina Hof Chardonnay.

Pistachio-crusted Salmon
with Cilantro Lime Cream

Serves 2

12	OUNCES SALMON FILLETS
2	OUNCES PISTACHIO NUTS
½	OUNCE BREAD CRUMBS
1	TABLESPOON FRESH BASIL, CHOPPED FINE
1	TABLESPOON FRESH MARJORAM, CHOPPED FINE
1	TEASPOON FRESH LIME JUICE
	SALT, TO TASTE
	FRESH GROUND BLACK PEPPER, TO TASTE
	CAYENNE PEPPER, TO TASTE

Place pistachios, bread crumbs, basil, marjoram, salt, and pepper in a food processor. Chop using the pulse feature (on and quickly off) until largest pistachio pieces are ¼ inch in size. Place mixture into a flat pan. Season salmon with salt, pepper, and lime juice. Firmly press seasoned salmon into pistachio mixture. Turn salmon over and repeat. Be sure salmon is completely covered with pistachio mixture. Place salmon in a non-stick baking dish and bake at 350° for 8–10 minutes or until salmon is done; or sauté in a non-stick skillet with 1–2 tablespoons olive oil on medium heat until done. Place Cilantro Lime Cream sauce on plate, and put Pistachio Crusted Salmon on top of sauce. Garnish with sprigs of fresh cilantro.

Cilantro Lime Cream Sauce with Fall Creek Vineyards Chenin Blanc

¼   CUP FALL CREEK CHENIN BLANC

5   OUNCES HEAVY CREAM

1   TABLESPOON GARLIC, CHOPPED

1   TABLESPOON SHALLOT, CHOPPED

1   TABLESPOON SEASONED SALT, OR SALT AND PEPPER, TO TASTE

2   TABLESPOONS FRESH CILANTRO, CHOPPED

    JUICE OF ¼ LIME

Pour first six ingredients into sauté pan, and cook over medium heat until thick. Remove from heat, add lime juice, and check for seasoning.

Courtesy of Charles Watkins, owner and chef, Sierra Grill, Houston. Serve with Fall Creek Vineyards Chenin Blanc.

Seared Tuna on Wasabi Mashers with Grilled Shiitakes, Ginger Slaw and Lemongrass Broth

Serves 6

6   SIX OUNCES TUNA FILLETS

6   OUNCES PONZU MARINADE, RECIPE FOLLOWS

Marinate tuna 5–10 minutes. Remove from marinade and keep cold.

Wasabi Mashers

2   POUNDS IDAHO POTATOES, PEELED AND QUARTERED

1 ½   TABLESPOONS WASABI, MIXED WITH 1 TABLESPOON
      WATER TO FORM PASTE

    LEMON JUICE

    SWEET BUTTER

½   CUP HEAVY CREAM

½   CUP MILK

2   TEASPOONS KOSHER SALT

Put the potatoes in a 2-quart saucepan with 1 teaspoon of the salt and cold water to cover. Bring to a boil, then lower the heat, cover and simmer until tender, about 30 minutes. Test with knife for doneness. Drain in a colander, and allow to dry on a flat pan in a warm oven. Lightly heat cream and milk, and add butter when warm.

Pass the potatoes through a potato ricer or food mill, or mash by hand. Place the potatoes over low heat and, with a wooden spoon, begin beating in the warm milk mixture, wasabi, and lemon juice. Season with remaining salt and serve promptly. Mashers are best served right away, but you can keep them warm in a double boiler for up to an hour.

Grilled (or Oven-Roasted) Shiitake Mushrooms

18   SHIITAKE CAPS, DE-STEMMED

8   OUNCES PONZU MARINADE

Preheat grill or oven to 400°. Rinse shiitake caps in cold water and marinate 10 minutes in Ponzu. Place on grill and cook 2–3 minutes each side, or roast in a 400°oven for 10–15 minutes until cooked through. Set aside for later use.

Ponzu Marinade

½   CUP SOY, PREFERABLY WHITE

½   CUP WATER

2   CLOVES GARLIC, MINCED

1   1″ PIECE GINGER ROOT, GRATED

    JUICE OF 2 LEMONS

Combine all and keep sealed and refrigerated up to 1 month.

Ginger Slaw

½   HEAD RED OR WHITE CABBAGE, THINLY SLICED

1   OUNCE PICKLED GINGER, MINCED, AND 1 OUNCE JUICE

2   OUNCES RICE VINEGAR

2   TABLESPOONS SUGAR

½   TEASPOON SESAME OIL

¼   TEASPOON BLACK SESAME SEEDS

½   TEASPOON SALT

Combine all in bowl and let sit at least 6 hours, preferably overnight.

Lemongrass Broth

1½	QUARTS CHICKEN OR LOBSTER STOCK, COLD
1	POUND GROUND CHICKEN OR FIRM FISH
1	CARROT, MINCED
2	CELERY RIBS, MINCED
1	MEDIUM ONION, MINCED
4	CLOVES GARLIC, MINCED
1	1½″ PIECE GINGER, MINCED
3	STALKS LEMONGRASS, MINCED
6	KAFFIR LIME LEAVES, MINCED (OR ½ TEASPOON LIME JUICE)
6	EGG WHITES

Place cold chicken or lobster stock in 2-quart saucepan. Combine remaining ingredients in bowl. Place ingredients in cold stock and stir lightly. Place over medium heat, and stir twice before it comes up to a light simmer. Reduce heat and simmer 30 minutes. Remove from heat, strain carefully through cheesecloth, and keep warm.

Final Assembly

½	POUND BEAN SPROUTS
3	SCALLIONS, SLICED INTO RINGS
2	JULIENNED BABY BOK CHOY
1	JULIENNED BELL PEPPER
1	JULIENNED CARROT
½	BUNCH FRESH CHOPPED CILANTRO AND SPRIGS
	SALT AND PEPPER
	ZEST OF 1 LEMON

Bring heavy skillet or comal to a high heat. It is very important to have your pan very, very hot to sear properly. Place tuna fillet on skillet and sear approximately 2–3 minutes per side. While tuna is cooking, heat broth with ingredients above. Add lemon zest and season with salt and pepper.

Place mashers in a shallow bowl. Place cooked tuna on mashers, pour a little broth with vegetables over tuna, and garnish with chopped cilantro. Top tuna with slaw and cilantro sprig.

❧ Courtesy of Bruce Auden, owner and chef, Restaurant BIGA, San Antonio. Serve with Sister Creek Chardonnay.

Shrimp Fiesta

Serves 4–6

12	OUNCES MESSINA HOF WHITE ZINFANDEL
½	ONION
1	SPRIG PARSLEY
	JUICE OF 1 LEMON
1	BAY LEAF
1	TEASPOON SALT
2	POUNDS RAW SHRIMP, PEELED AND DEVEINED
2	TABLESPOONS BUTTER
2	TABLESPOONS FLOUR
8	OUNCES TOMATO SAUCE
¼	CUP CHOPPED SCALLIONS
¼	TEASPOON HOT PEPPER
¼	TEASPOON NUTMEG
	PINCH OF SUGAR

Bring wine, onion, parsley, lemon, bay leaf, and salt to a boil. Add shrimp and bring to boil again. Simmer for 5 minutes. Drain and save liquid. Melt butter in skillet. Stir in flour until bubbly. Stir in shrimp liquid and rest of ingredients until mixture boils and thickens slightly. Stir in shrimp and heat thoroughly. Serve with hot buttered noodles.

❧ Courtesy of Messina Hof Wine Cellars. Serve with Messina Hof White Zinfandel

Sicilian Seafood Platter

Serves 6

1	DOZEN OYSTERS
2	POUNDS WHITING FILLETS
6	LOBSTER TAILS
1	POUND CODFISH, COOKED AND SHREDDED
3	EGGS
2	CUPS BREAD CRUMBS SEASONED WITH SALT, PEPPER, GRATED ROMANO CHEESE, AND FLOUR
½	CUP WATER
1	CLOVE MINCED GARLIC
2	TABLESPOONS BASIL
2	TABLESPOONS MINCED PARSLEY
1	CUP RAISINS
	PAPA PAULO PORT
1	LEMON
6	SPRIGS OF PARSLEY
	OLIVE OIL

Drain oysters, coat with flour, dip in one egg (well beaten), and dredge in seasoned bread crumbs and minced parsley. Pan fry in olive oil over low heat until golden brown, and place in baking dish. Prepare whiting in same fashion, and place in baking dish. Boil lobster tails for about 15 minutes. Cool under running cold water. Remove meat from undershells, cut into bitesize pieces, and place in baking dish.

Place codfish in baking dish. Beat 2 egg yolks and add ½ cup water and a sprinkle of olive oil; season with garlic clove, salt, pepper, grated Romano cheese, basil, and minced parsley. Pour over contents in baking dish. Add a cup of bread crumbs, raisins, and enough Port to cover. Bake at 350° for about 30 minutes. Garnish with lemon wedges and 6 sprigs of parsley.

Courtesy of Messina Hof Wine Cellars.
Serve with Messina Hof Sauvignon Blanc.

Skewered Shrimp

"Scampi is a shellfish native to the waters of the Adriatic, but jumbo shrimp will do nicely. They are packed on skewers, broiled and basted simply with salad oil, then dashed with lemon juice and parsley when ready to serve." —Merrill Bonarrigo, Messina Hof Wine Cellars.

Serves 4

20	JUMBO SHRIMP
	WAFER-THIN SLICES OF CANADIAN BACON OR HAM
1	TABLESPOON MESSINA HOF PAPA PAULO PORT
½	CUP MESSINA HOF CHENIN BLANC
⅓	CUP CONSOMMÉ
2	TEASPOONS LEMON JUICE
2	TEASPOONS MINCED PARSLEY
½	TEASPOON WORCESTERSHIRE SAUCE
	DASH CAYENNE PEPPER
	SALT
	OLIVE OIL

Shell and devein shrimp, leaving tails intact. Rinse and pat dry on paper towels. On each of 4 skewers thread 5 shrimp alternately with small rolled bacon or ham, piercing shrimp so sides lie flat in pan. Brown lightly in hot olive oil on each side. Sprinkle with Port and add rest of the ingredients. Cover lightly; simmer gently about 5 minutes. Remove to warm plates. Pour sauce over shrimp.

Courtesy of Messina Hof Wine Cellars.
Serve with Messina Hof Chenin Blanc.

Smoked Tomato and Crab Rissoto

2   QUARTS DOUBLE CHICKEN BROTH, WARM OR CLAM AND MUSSEL SERRANO CILANTRO BROTH (RECIPES FOLLOW)

2   POUNDS PLUM TOMATOES, SMOKED, PURÉED

4   TABLESPOONS UNSALTED BUTTER

1   MEDIUM ONION, DICED

3   CUPS ARBORIO RICE

½   TEASPOON KOSHER SALT

¼   TEASPOON GROUND PEPPER

   JUICE OF LEMON

2   CLOVES GARLIC, MINCED

1   CUP LLANO ESTACADO SIGNATURE WHITE

2   TABLESPOONS ITALIAN PARSLEY, CHOPPED

2   CUPS ROMANO CHEESE, GRATED

½   POUND LUMP CRAB MEAT FROM BLUE CRABS

Heat half the butter in a 5–6 quart casserole over medium heat. Add the onion and sauté about 8 minutes, until translucent. Add the garlic and sauté an additional 3–4 minutes. Add the rice and stir over medium heat for 3 minutes, until a small dot appears in the center of the kernels. Stir in the wine and simmer until dry. Pour 1 cup stock and smoked tomatoes just to barely cover the rice, stirring frequently until absorbed by the rice. Add the remaining stock, 1 cup at a time, stirring each addition until it is absorbed. After about six cups of stock have been added, check the rice for doneness. It should be chewy, not crunchy. Season with salt and pepper. Add remaining butter. Remove from heat and add chopped parsley and 1 cup of Romano. If rice is not creamy, add another ½ cup of hot stock. Fold in crab meat. Keep warm until ready to serve. Serve with Double Chicken Broth or Clam and Mussel Serrano Cilantro Broth.

Double Chicken Broth for Rissoto

3	QUARTS CHICKEN STOCK
3	POUNDS CHICKEN BONES, NECKS, GIZZARDS, WINGS, ETC., CUT IN SMALL PIECES
1	CUP FALL CREEK VINEYARDS SAUVIGNON BLANC
2	CARROTS, DICED
1	STALK CELERY, DICED
1	MEDIUM ONION, DICED
1	STALK LEMONGRASS, SMASHED
1	HEAD GARLIC, SPLIT IN HALF
3	BAY LEAVES
6	SPRIGS LEMON THYME
3	SPRIGS ITALIAN PARSLEY

Place all ingredients in large stockpot. Bring to a boil, reduce to a simmer. Allow to simmer 1½ to 2 hours, skimming broth occasionally. Strain and cook in ice bath. May be prepared ahead of time and kept in refrigerator 3–4 days or frozen in ice cube trays (covered) up to 3 months.

Clam and Mussel Serrano Cilantro Broth

1	TABLESPOON UNSALTED BUTTER
4	MINCED SHALLOTS
3	CLOVES MINCED GARLIC
10	CHOPPED TOMATILLOS
6	CHOPPED SERRANO PEPPERS
1	CUP LLANO ESTACADO SIGNATURE WHITE
1	CUP CHICKEN STOCK
24	MANILA CLAMS
16	MUSSELS, PREFERABLY FROM WASHINGTON STATE
1	BUNCH CILANTRO, MOSTLY LEAVES
4	LEAVES FRESH SPINACH
	JUICE OF 1 LIME
	SALT AND PEPPER, TO TASTE

Place butter in a 4-quart saucepan over medium heat. Add shallots and garlic; sauté 4–5 minutes. Add chopped tomatillos and sauté another 3–4 minutes. Add serranos and wine, and simmer 3–4 minutes. Add chicken stock, clams, and mussels.

Cover pan and turn heat to medium high. Shellfish will open in about 5–10 minutes. Remove shellfish from broth and keep warm.

Add cilantro, spinach, and lime juice to broth. Purée in blender. Return to saucepan and season with salt and pepper.

Bring to a quick boil. Remove from heat and pour over shellfish.

❧ *Courtesy of Mark Bliss, Chef de Cuisine, Restaurant BIGA, San Antonio. Serve with Fall Creek Vineyards Sauvignon Blanc-Semillon.*

Sweet Chili Shrimp with Roasted Garlic Beurre Blanc

1	TABLESPOON GARLIC, ROASTED
¼	CUP FALL CREEK CHENIN BLANC
1	TABLESPOON LIME JUICE
1	TABLESPOON CHOPPED SHALLOT
1	TEASPOON GARLIC
¼	CUP HEAVY CREAM
½	POUND BUTTER, SALTED
	WHITE PEPPER, TO TASTE
1	TABLESPOON LIME JUICE
	BASIL OR CILANTRO, TO GARNISH

Roasted Garlic Beurre Blanc

To roast garlic, chop and place in sauté pan with a little butter. Cook until dark brown. Reserve.

Place wine, lime juice, shallots, and garlic in a saucepan, and cook over medium heat 3–4 minutes. Add heavy cream and cook 2–3 more minutes. Remove from heat and begin beating in butter a little at a time with a wire whisk. Continue until all butter is incorporated. Add additional tablespoon lime juice, roasted garlic, and white pepper to taste. Reserve.

Shrimp

18   LARGE SHRIMP

6   OUNCES SWEET RED PEPPERS, FLAKED

    SALT AND PEPPER

Place sweet chili flakes on a plate. Season shrimp with salt and pepper, then press firmly into chili flakes, coating evenly. Bake or sauté shrimp until done. Place shrimp on plate and spoon garlic beurre blanc sauce over shrimp. Garnish with fine chopped basil or cilantro.

❧ *Courtesy of Charles Watkins, owner and chef Sierra Grill, Houston. Serve with Fall Creek Vineyards Chenin Blanc.*

Tequila Fillet Sauté

Serves 6

6   FILLETS OF FISH (SNAPPER, SOLE, FLOUNDER OR ANY WHITE FLESH FISH)

½   CUP MILK

½   CUP FLOUR (OR AS NEEDED TO COAT FISH)

    SALT, TO TASTE

1   TABLESPOON, OR TO TASTE, OF CHOLULU HOT SAUCE

1½   TABLESPOON BUTTER AND VEGETABLE OIL

Place the fillets in a glass dish in one layer. Pour milk and Cholulu hot sauce over and let rest for 15 minutes or longer.

Mound flour seasoned with salt on a piece of waxed paper or flat dish.

When ready to sauté, remove fillets from milk, but don't drain; coat with flour on both sides.

Sauté in butter and vegetable oil over medium heat about 2–3 minutes per side, depending on thickness. (It takes 10 minutes to cook a 1″ thick fillet).

Sauce

12	TABLESPOONS BUTTER
½	CUP TEQUILA
2	CLOVES MINCED GARLIC
¼	CUP CHOPPED GREEN ONION
2	TABLESPOONS LIME JUICE
2	TABLESPOONS CHOLULU HOT SAUCE (OR MORE TO TASTE)
2	TABLESPOONS CAPERS
2	TABLESPOONS PARSLEY

Heat 4 tablespoons butter on medium heat in a saucepot or skillet until it begins to color. When butter is bubbly and golden, add minced garlic and scallions, lower temperature, and add tequila. Cook for a minute or two until it begins to thicken. Add lime juice and Cholulu hot sauce. Over *very low* heat, whisk in remaining 8 tablespoons butter, 1 tablespoon at a time. Sauce will thicken to satiny consistency. Stir in capers and minced parsley, and serve over fish fillets.

❧ *Courtesy of John Rydman, Spec's Liquor Stores, Houston. Serve with Slaughter-Leftwich Vineyards Chenin Blanc.*

Texas Creole Barbecue Shrimp with Texas Cornbread Pudding and Jicama Salad

Shrimp

Serves 4

16	SHRIMP, PEELED
¾	CUP BARBECUE SAUCE BASE, RECIPE FOLLOWS
¼	CUP WHIPPING CREAM
⅓	CUP RED BELL PEPPER, JULIENNED
⅓	CUP POBLANO PEPPER, JULIENNED
⅓	CUP YELLOW ONION, JULIENNED
¾	TEASPOON GARLIC
½	TABLESPOON VEGETABLE OIL

Sauté red bell pepper, poblano, onion, and garlic in a skillet for about 30–40 seconds. Next add shrimp and sauté for 30 seconds. Add barbecue sauce base and bring to a simmer. Add cream and simmer until shrimp are cooked.

Spoon shrimp and sauce onto plate, and serve with cornbread pudding and jicama salad.

Barbecue Shrimp Sauce Base

2½	LEMONS, PEELED AND QUARTERED
3	TABLESPOONS COARSELY GROUND BLACK PEPPER
2	TABLESPOONS SEAFOOD SEASONING
1	CUP WORCESTERSHIRE SAUCE
1	CUP WATER
6	CLOVES GARLIC

In a saucepan, combine all ingredients and reduce by half. Strain off liquid and use for barbecue shrimp. Adjust spiciness of sauce by increasing or decreasing to your taste.

Jicama Salad

1½	CUPS JICAMA, PEELED AND JULIENNED
	JUICE OF 1 LIME
	SALT, TO TASTE
	GROUND BLACK PEPPER, TO TASTE

Season jicama with lime juice, salt and pepper. The jicama will give a refreshing taste with the spicy shrimp.

Texas Cornbread Pudding

½   CUP YELLOW ONIONS, DICED

1½   CUPS CORN

1   TABLESPOON VEGETABLE OIL

4   EGGS

2   CUPS WHIPPING CREAM

1   QUART CORNBREAD

1   JALAPEÑO, SLICED THIN

1   CUP JALAPEÑO JACK CHEESE, SHREDDED

Sauté onions and corn in oil until onions are translucent.

Combine eggs, cream, ½ cup jalapeño cheese, cornbread, onions, and corn. Season to taste with salt and pepper.

Butter or spray an 8″ × 8″ × 2″ pan. Pour in custard mixture. Sprinkle top with remaining ½ cup of jalapeño cheese and jalapeño slices.

Set pan in water bath and bake at 300° for 1 hour or until firm.

❧ *Courtesy of Alex Brennan-Martin, owner, Brennan's Restaurant, Houston. Serve with Fall Creek Vineyards Chardonnay.*

WALNUT CREEK CE
VINTAGE
1984
TEXAS PORT
LIMITED BOTTLING
WIMBERLEY VALLE
HEASANT RIDGE
Messina Hof
PRIVATE RESERVE
Special Reserve
Poultry
Hill Country Cellars
SLAUGHTER LEFTWICH
VINEYARDS
AP ROCK
1994
CABERNET ROYALE
SÉ OF CABERNET SAUVIGNON
TEXAS
ALC 11% BY VOL
FALL CREEK
VINEYARDS
Grape
VINEY
LL MOUNTAIN
ESTATE BOTTLED
STE. GENEVIEVE
1994
TEXA
CHARDO

# The Bonarrigos' Fiesta Chicken Cacciatore

Serves 4

2	BROILER-FRYERS, QUARTERED
¾	CUP ALL-PURPOSE FLOUR
1	TABLESPOON SALT
¼	TEASPOON PEPPER
⅓	CUP OLIVE OIL
1	LARGE ONION, CHOPPED
1	CLOVE GARLIC, MINCED
1	CUP MESSINA HOF CHENIN BLANC
1	CAN ITALIAN TOMATOES
1	TABLESPOON SUGAR
1	TEASPOON BASIL, CHOPPED
½	TEASPOON THYME, CHOPPED
2	MEDIUM GREEN PEPPERS, HALVED, SEEDED AND SLICED

Shake chicken with flour, salt, and pepper in a plastic bag to coat well. Brown pieces, a few at a time, in olive oil. Remove and reserve.

Stir onion and garlic into drippings in pan, and sauté until soft. Stir in wine, tomatoes, sugar, basil, and thyme; bring to a boil. Return chicken to pan; spoon tomato sauce over top; place sliced green peppers on top.

Bake at 350° for 30 minutes.

*Courtesy of Merrill Bonarrigo, Messina Hof Wine Cellars.
Serve with Messina Hof Chenin Blanc.*

Boston Roast Duckling with Port Wine Sauce

Serves 2

2	5-POUND DUCKLINGS
3	TEASPOONS SALT
6	WHOLE BLACK PEPPERS
2	MEDIUM ONIONS, PEELED AND QUARTERED
2	ORANGES, PEELED
2	CUPS MESSINA HOF PAPA PAULO PORT
1	CELERY STALK, CUT UP
2	CARROTS, PARED AND CUT UP
1	CAN CHICKEN BROTH
¼	CUP ALL-PURPOSE FLOUR

Preheat oven to 425° Remove giblets and necks from ducklings; set aside for sauce. Sprinkle each duck inside and out with 1 teaspoon salt. Stuff cavity with 3 black peppers, onion, and orange.

Bring skin of neck over back; fasten with poultry pins. Close cavity of each with poultry pins. Tie ends of legs together. Prick skin around thighs and back. Place ducks, breast side up and side by side, on rack in a shallow roasting pan. Roast, uncovered, 20 minutes. Reduce oven temperature to 325° and roast 1 hour. Remove pan from oven; pour off fat. Pour port over ducklings; roast, basting occasionally, until skin is golden brown.

In a medium saucepan, place giblets and necks, celery, carrot, chicken broth, and 1 teaspoon salt. Bring to a boil; reduce heat and simmer, covered, for 2 hours. Remove giblets; discard necks. Chop giblets finely; set aside. Strain broth; reserve 1 cup, add giblets. Remove ducklings to warm serving platter; remove pins and twine. Keep warm until serving.

❀ Courtesy of Messina Hof Wine Cellars.
Serve with Messina Hof Cabernet Franc.

Chicken à la Bourguignonne

Serves 6–8

8	PIECES CHICKEN (BREASTS OR THIGHS)
2	SLICES BACON
1	LARGE ONION, SLICED
2	TABLESPOONS FLOUR
3	TABLESPOONS BUTTER
1	CUP PHEASANT RIDGE CABERNET SAUVIGNON
½	CUP WATER
8	OUNCES SLICED MUSHROOMS

Brown chicken pieces in butter with bacon and onions until golden. Sprinkle with flour and season with salt and pepper, if desired. Add the Pheasant Ridge wine and water. Mix until sauce is thickened. Cover and cook 30 minutes over low heat. Stir in mushrooms and cook an additional 15 minutes.

Courtesy of Bill Gipson, Sr., owner, Pheasant Ridge Winery.
Serve with Pheasant Ridge Cabernet Sauvignon.

Chicken and Spinach Enchiladas

*"What better food to serve with Texas Wine than Tex-Mex fare?
This recipe for chicken and spinach enchiladas has become quite
popular among my friends and family, and is always the requested
menu when I have guests for dinner. I serve it with black beans on
the side and a garnish of sour cream, chopped tomatoes and fresh
cilantro. This recipe makes two large (9" × 13") pans. I use one for
dinner and freeze the other for up to three months. You can also
substitute low-fat cheese and/or dairy products if you are counting
calories!"*–Mrs. Sandy Starr, Personnel Director, Gaido's
Restaurant, Galveston.

Sauce

Serves 12

1	CUP BUTTER
½	CUP FLOUR
6	CUPS WHOLE MILK
16	OUNCES CREAM CHEESE, CUT INTO 1" CUBES
16	OUNCES SOUR CREAM
3	LARGE JALAPEÑO PEPPERS, SEEDED AND FINELY DICED

Melt butter in a large, heavy saucepan. Stir in flour, cooking for about 1
minute. Slowly stir in milk. Continue cooking over medium heat, stirring
constantly until mixture thickens to coat spoon. Add cream cheese and
stir until melted. Remove from heat and fold in sour cream and jalapeños.

Filling

8	BONELESS, SKINLESS CHICKEN BREASTS, COOKED AND DICED
2	10-OUNCE PACKAGES FROZEN CHOPPED SPINACH, THAWED AND DRAINED
12	OUNCES COTTAGE CHEESE
16	OUNCES SHREDDED MONTEREY JACK CHEESE
¼	CUP FINELY DICED FRESH CILANTRO
2	LARGE JALAPEÑO PEPPERS, SEEDED AND FINELY DICED
2	CUPS OF SAUCE FROM PRECEDING RECIPE (RESERVE REMAINDER FOR FUTURE USE)
	FLOUR TORTILLAS

Combine first six ingredients. Toss until well blended. Stir in just enough sauce to bind ingredients. Spoon a scant ¼ cup of filling into a flour tortilla. Roll enchilada and place seam side down in 9″ × 13″ pan. Fill both pans, then divide sauce evenly over tops of tortillas. Top each pan with additional shredded Monterey Jack cheese. Bake at 350° for 20–25 minutes or until lightly browned. Serve immediately with extra flour tortillas on the side.

❧ *Serve with Fall Creek Vineyards Chardonnay.*

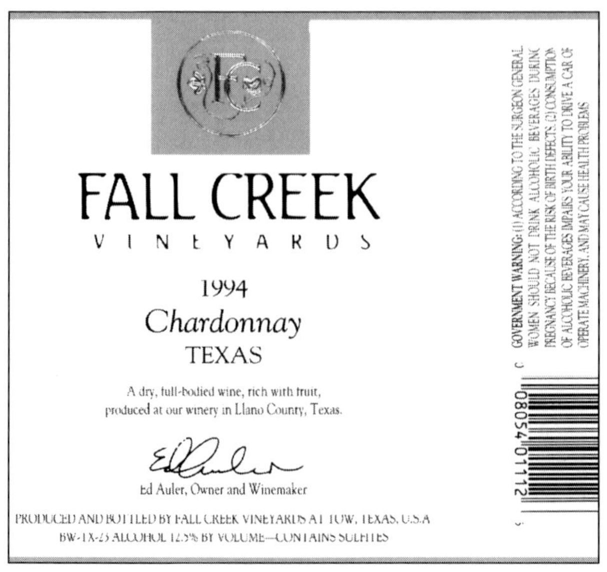

Chicken Breasts with Curry Sauce

Serves 4

4	CHICKEN BREASTS, DEBONED
2	TABLESPOONS BUTTER
¾	TEASPOON SWEET BASIL
1	STALK CELERY, CHOPPED INTO BITE-SIZED PIECES
5	TABLESPOONS Riesling
	SALT TO TASTE
	CURRY SAUCE, RECIPE FOLLOWS
4	FLOUR TORTILLAS, WARMED

Melt butter in skillet. Place chicken in butter, sprinkle sweet basil over breasts. Sauté breasts over medium heat, about 6–7 minutes per side.

Add the chopped celery and cook for about 1 minute; it should be crisp.

Add Riesling, scraping the skillet carefully, and heat gently for about 1 minute.

Curry Sauce

2	TABLESPOONS BUTTER
2	TABLESPOONS ONION, FINELY CHOPPED
1½–2	TEASPOONS CURRY POWDER*
2	CUPS MILK
¾	TEASPOON SALT, OR TO TASTE
2	TABLESPOONS CORNSTARCH
3	TABLESPOONS Riesling

Curry powders vary in intensity and flavor. Go lightly and taste as you proceed.

Melt butter. Add curry powder and cook over low heat for 30 seconds. Add onion; cook for about a minute, adding 1 tablespoon wine for liquid. Remove from heat and add 1¾ cup milk; blend.

Mix cornstarch with remaining ¼ cup milk until smooth. Add cornstarch mixture to the curry mixture. Return to medium heat; add salt and remaining wine. Heat, stirring constantly until thickened, about 2–3 minutes.

To serve, place one breast onto a tortilla and spoon curry sauce over it. Garnish with fresh parsley or sweet basil leaf.

❧ *Courtesy of Shirley Jones, Southwest editor of* American Wine on the Web. *Serve with your favorite Texas Riesling.*

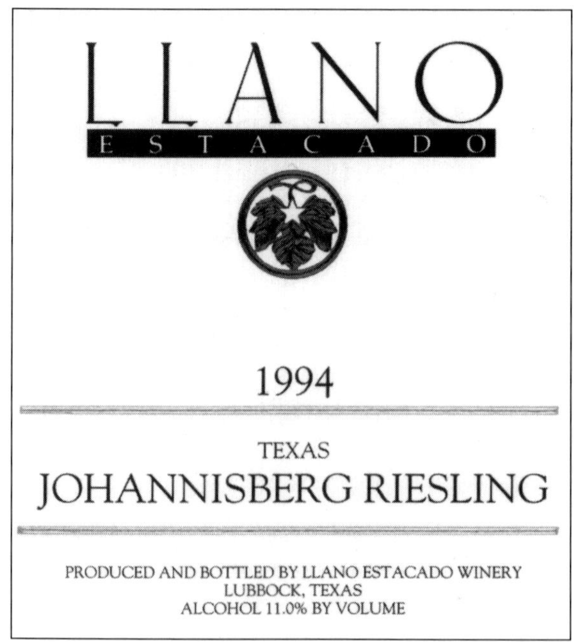

Christi's Sautéed Chicken Strips

2	WHOLE CHICKEN BREASTS, SPLIT, BONED, AND SKINNED
½	TEASPOON EACH SALT AND FRESH GROUND PEPPER
4	TEASPOONS EACH CORNSTARCH AND OIL
1	EGG WHITE
6	TABLESPOONS BUTTER
½	CUP MINCED FRESH PARSLEY
¼	CUP MINCED CHIVES

Slice chicken diagonally in ½″ strips. Place in a bowl and toss with salt and pepper. Let stand for 20 minutes. Sprinkle with cornstarch and oil; turn with spoon to coat. Let stand for 20 minutes. Fold in egg white. Let stand for 30 minutes.

Heat butter in heavy skillet on medium heat, until it bubbles and begins to brown. Add chicken strips and sauté 4–5 minutes, until just opaque throughout and lightly golden. Fold in parsley and chives, and remove immediately to warm serving dish.

*Courtesy of Mary Beth and John Bratcher, Vice President of Sales and Marketing, Cap*Rock Winery.*
*Serve with Cap*Rock Chardonnay.*

Fried Chicken and Cream Gravy

Serves 4

1	FRESH CHICKEN, ABOUT 2½–3 POUNDS
2	CUPS BUTTERMILK
	SALT AND BLACK PEPPER
	CAYENNE PEPPER, OPTIONAL
2	CUPS PLUS 2½ TABLESPOONS FLOUR
3–4	CUPS VEGETABLE SHORTENING, OR A COMBINATION OF LARD AND SHORTENING
2	CUPS MILK
1	TABLESPOON CHOPPED PARSLEY, OPTIONAL

Cut up chicken into pieces as follows: two thighs, two drumsticks, two wings (tips removed), the wishbone, two breast halves, and, if desired, the back containing the "oysters."

Put buttermilk in a pan large enough to hold the chicken in one layer. Mix in 1 teaspoon salt, ½ teaspoon black pepper, and ¼ teaspoon cayenne, if desired. Add chicken pieces, coat thoroughly, and cover the pan with plastic wrap. Refrigerate 2 hours or overnight.

Put 2 cups of flour in a paper or plastic bag and season with 2 teaspoons salt, 1 teaspoon black pepper, and ½ teaspoon cayenne, if desired. Drain chicken pieces and toss, one at a time, in the flour mixture. Heat shortening in a 12″ cast-iron skillet so that it reaches a depth of about ½ inch. (You might need two skillets, or you can do the chicken in batches, keeping the cooked pieces warm in a low oven.)

When hot but not smoking (no more than 375°), add chicken pieces, making sure that the pan is not crowded. (Make sure the fat bubbles, indicating it is hot enough.) Cook chicken evenly on all sides until nicely browned. Then reduce heat to medium-low.

At this point you can cover the pan if you wish. Cook, turning pieces periodically, until the chicken is cooked through. Total cooking time is 15–22 minutes, depending on the size of the pieces.

Remove the cooked chicken to drain on paper bags, paper towels, or a clean wire rack over a sheet pan. Pour out all but 2 tablespoons of fat from the pan, saving the browned bits that have accumulated on the bottom. Add 2½ tablespoons flour and, over medium heat, combine with the fat to make a roux. Whisk in milk and combine thoroughly while bringing the gravy to simmer a few minutes, or until the sauce is thickened and there is no flour taste. Season with salt and pepper, and add chopped parsley if desired. Pour gravy over biscuits and mashed potatoes.

✲ Courtesy of Leigh Burns, Tasting Room Manager, Hill Country Cellars. Serve with Hill Country Cellars Sauvignon Blanc .

Italian Chicken with White Wine Sauce

8	BONELESS, SKINLESS CHICKEN BREAST HALVES	Serves 6
3	TABLESPOONS FAT-FREE ITALIAN DRESSING	
1	CLOVE OF GARLIC, MINCED	
1	TABLESPOON DIJON MUSTARD	
1	TABLESPOON HONEY	
2	TABLESPOONS CAPERS	
1	TABLESPOON CORNSTARCH	
1	TEASPOON LEMON PEPPER	
1	TEASPOON SALT	
¾	CUP STE. GENEVIEVE CHARDONNAY	

Marinate chicken in above ingredients 2 hours; save cornstarch and ¼ cup of wine for final sauce. Pour chicken into large non-stick skillet, and cook over medium-high heat for 10 minutes, turning chicken occasionally. Cover, lower heat to medium, and simmer 10 minutes. Remove chicken from skillet. Stir in cornstarch and remaining wine. Whisk until smooth. Cook over medium-high heat for 3–5 minutes. Pour wine sauce over chicken and serve over a bed of angel hair pasta.

✲ Courtesy of Don Brady, Winemaker, Ste. Genevieve Vineyards. Serve with Ste. Genevieve Chardonnay.

Nonna's Chicken Au Vin with Frozen Green Peas

Serves 4–6

6–8	CHICKEN BREASTS
¼	CUP BUTTER
1	MEDIUM CLOVE GARLIC, FINELY MINCED
2	TEASPOONS SALT
	DASH PEPPER
1	TEASPOON BASIL
½	CUP Messina Hof Chardonnay
1½	CUPS SLICED FRESH MUSHROOMS (ABOUT 5 OUNCES)
1	PACKAGE (10 OUNCES) FROZEN GREEN PEAS, PARTIALLY DEFROSTED
¼	CUP SLICED GREEN ONIONS
1	CUP HALF AND HALF
1	EGG, SLIGHTLY BEATEN
2	TABLESPOONS FLOUR

Brown chicken in butter over low heat, turning as needed to brown all sides. Sprinkle with garlic, 1 teaspoon salt, pepper, and basil. Add wine, cover, and cook slowly until chicken is fork tender, 30–40 minutes. Remove chicken from fry pan.

Add mushrooms, peas, and onion to wine mixture. Cover and simmer slowly until peas are tender, about 5 minutes. Combine half and half, egg, flour, and 1 teaspoon salt. Pour over pea-mushroom mixture, and cook until sauce is slightly thickened, stirring constantly. Serve over chicken.

Courtesy of Merrill Bonarrigo, Messina Hof Wine Cellars. Serve with Messina Hof Chardonnay.

Pecan Chicken

4	BONELESS CHICKEN BREASTS
1	POUND PACKAGE SUN-DRIED APRICOTS
½	CUP LLANO ESTACADO JOHANNISBERG RIESLING
1½	CUPS CHICKEN BROTH
2	TEASPOONS TOMATO PASTE
3	TEASPOONS DIJON MUSTARD
4	OUNCES TOASTED PECAN PIECES
	OLIVE OIL

Pound out chicken breast until flat, and slice into four medallions per breast. Place in seasoned flour and set aside.

Place apricots in a shallow bowl. Mix the wine and ½ cup of broth in a saucepan and heat to a boil. Pour the heated mixture over the apricots and let sit for 15 minutes.

Pour the liquid into pan, add in the remaining chicken broth, stir and simmer for 5 minutes. Add the tomato paste and Dijon mustard, stirring until blended. Simmer for another 5 minutes.

Add the apricots to the saucepan and coat well with the mixture. Simmer for 3 minutes.

While the sauce is simmering, heat a pan with olive oil and sauté the chicken medallions until cooked and light golden brown in color. Arrange cooked medallions on the plates, and top with sauce and apricots. Sprinkle the toasted pecan pieces over the top of the chicken and sauce.

❧ *Courtesy of Bill Delassandro, Food Consultant for Llano Estacado Winery, Lubbock.*
Serve with Llano Estacado Johannisberg Riesling.

Pheasant Ridge Chicken

Serves 6–8

6–8   BONELESS SKINLESS CHICKEN BREASTS

1   10¾ OUNCE CAN CREAM OF MUSHROOM SOUP

1   STICK BUTTER OR MARGARINE

1   CUP PHEASANT RIDGE VINTNER'S CUVÉE CHARDONNAY

8   OUNCES SOUR CREAM

    SALT AND PEPPER TO TASTE

Melt butter or margarine in skillet. Salt and pepper chicken and cook in butter until it turns white. Remove chicken from skillet and place in glass casserole dish. To the drippings in skillet, add cream of mushroom soup, sour cream, and wine; stir until blended. Pour over chicken. Cover and bake at 350° for 1–1½ hours. Serve over wild rice.

Courtesy of Bill Gipson, Sr., owner, Pheasant Ridge Winery.

Red River Rooster and Rice

4	SKINLESS, BONELESS ROOSTER (OR CHICKEN) BREASTS
2	CLOVES OF GARLIC, CRUSHED
1	MEDIUM ONION, DICED
1	SMALL RED BELL PEPPER, JULIENNED
1	SMALL YELLOW BELL PEPPER, JULIENNED
1	SMALL GREEN BELL PEPPER, JULIENNED
1	CUP TEXAS RED WINE (CABERNET)
2	CUPS ROOSTER (OR CHICKEN) BROTH
1	CUP WILD RICE
2	TABLESPOONS CHILI POWDER
1	TEASPOON CUMIN POWDER
8	TABLESPOONS OLIVE OIL
	SALT AND PEPPER TO TASTE

Place olive oil, crushed garlic, and diced onion in large skillet. Cook mixture on medium heat until onions are clear.

Cut rooster breasts in 1-inch strips and add to skillet. Add chili powder and cumin. Cook breasts on medium heat in mixture with lid on until breasts have been cooked throughout. Stir frequently.

Add red wine and rooster broth to skillet. Bring to a boil and add wild rice. Simmer with lid on until rice is tender. Do not stir.

Add red, green, and yellow bell pepper strips to rice and rooster mixture and stir. Cover skillet and continue to cook on low heat until peppers are tender. Salt and pepper to taste.

Garnish each serving with chopped cilantro.

❧ *Courtesy of Dr. Roy Renfro, Red River Valley Vineyards, Inc., and the T. V. Munson Memorial Vineyards.*
Serve with your favorite Texas Cabernet Sauvignon.

Skillet Chicken and Veggies in White Wine Sauce

Serves 4–6

1	CAN (ABOUT 10 OUNCES) CHICKEN BROTH
1	CUP DELANEY VINEYARDS TEXAS WHITE TABLE WINE
1	TABLESPOON FRESH MINCED ONION
½	TEASPOON SALT
1	BAY LEAF
¼	TEASPOON ROSEMARY, CRUSHED
6	HALF BREASTS OF CHICKEN
6	SMALL CARROTS
6	SMALL ZUCCHINI
2	TABLESPOONS CORNSTARCH
2	TABLESPOONS COLD WATER
3	TABLESPOONS CHOPPED PIMENTO
2	TABLESPOONS CHOPPED CILANTRO OR PARSLEY

Combine broth, wine, onion, salt, bay leaf, and rosemary in large skillet. Heat to boiling. Place chicken breasts in boiling liquid; cover and simmer 20 minutes. While chicken is cooking, pare carrots and cut in half lengthwise. Cut zucchini in half lengthwise. Add carrots and zucchini to the chicken; cover and cook 15 minutes more, or until chicken is tender and veggies are crisp/tender. Remove chicken and vegetables with slotted spoon; keep warm. Mix cornstarch with water and stir into liquid remaining in skillet. Cook, stirring until sauce boils thoroughly. Add pimento and cilantro, and pour over chicken on serving dish. Serve immediately.

❧ *Courtesy of Mary Burge, wife of Stu Burge, Executive Director, Texas Grape Growers Association, Colleyville.*
Serve with Delaney Vineyards Texas White Table Wine.

Sour Cream Enchiladas

2	CHICKEN BREASTS, HALVED, SKINLESS, BONELESS
1	10¾ OUNCE CAN CREAM OF MUSHROOM SOUP
8	OUNCES SOUR CREAM
1	ONION, CHOPPED
4½	CUPS MONTEREY JACK CHEESE, GRATED (WITH JALAPEÑOS, IF AVAILABLE)
1	4-OUNCE CAN GREEN CHILIES, CHOPPED
	SALT, BLACK PEPPER, AND LEMON PEPPER TO TASTE
12	FLOUR TORTILLAS

1. Boil chicken breasts with 1 teaspoon lemon pepper until done. Save broth, keep warm.
2. Shred chicken.
3. In saucepan, sauté onion in margarine or cooking spray.
4. In same pan, over low heat, mix onion, soup, sour cream, chilies, salt, pepper, and lemon pepper for sauce. Keep warm.
5. Dip tortilla in warm broth, shake off excess.
6. Fill with chicken, spoon in sauce, and top with grated cheese. Reserve some chicken, cheese, and sauce.
7. Roll tortilla tightly and place in dish.
8. Continue until dish is full or all tortillas are used.
9. Top filled dish with reserved chicken, cheese, and sauce.
10. Bake at 350° for 30–45 minutes or until cheese is bubbling and beginning to brown.

*Courtesy of Kim Powell, Operations Manager, Cap*Rock Winery. Serve with Cap*Rock Chardonnay.*

Stir-fried Chicken with Shiitake Mushrooms and Jicama

Serves 4

1	POUND SKINLESS, BONELESS CHICKEN BREASTS
1	TABLESPOON CORNSTARCH
1	TABLESPOON SAKE OR DRY SHERRY
½	TEASPOON SUGAR
2½	TABLESPOONS PEANUT OIL
2	OUNCES COOKED HAM, JULIENNED (1″ × ⅛″) STRIPS
1	TEASPOON MINCED FRESH GINGER ROOT
1	GARLIC CLOVE, MINCED
¼	POUND WELL-RINSED, FRESH SHIITAKE MUSHROOMS OR 12 DRIED* SHIITAKES, CUT INTO ⅛ INCH SLIVERS
3	TABLESPOONS CHICKEN BROTH OR WATER
1	CUP JICAMA, JULIENNED (1″× ⅛″)
1	TABLESPOON CHINESE OYSTER SAUCE
1	TABLESPOON CHINESE MUSHROOM SOY, LIGHT SOY, OR IMPORTED JAPANESE SOY SAUCE
1	TEASPOON ORIENTAL SESAME OIL
⅓	CUP THINLY SLICED SCALLIONS

Prepare the chicken. Trim away and discard any fat and tendons from the chicken breasts. Wrap and partially freeze to facilitate slicing; the chicken should be firm but not frozen solid. Cut the chicken on the bias into thin slices. Toss in a bowl with the cornstarch, sake, and sugar. Marinate at room temperature for 20 minutes.

In a wok or large heavy skillet, warm 2 tablespoons of peanut oil over moderately high heat. Add the ham and stir-fry until it begins to curl, 1½–2 minutes. Add the chicken and any remaining marinade, and stir-fry until the chicken turns opaque, 2–3 minutes. Remove the ham and chicken from the wok and reserve.

Add remaining peanut oil to the wok along with the ginger and garlic; stir-fry for 15 seconds. Stir in the mushrooms and the broth. Reduce the heat to low, cover and cook 2–3 minutes, until the mushrooms wilt. Uncover, add the jicama and cook, stirring for 30 seconds.

Raise the heat to moderately high, and stir in the reserved chicken and ham. Add the oyster sauce, soy, sesame oil, and scallions. Stir-fry for 30 seconds and serve.

*If using dried shiitake mushrooms, first soak them in warm water for 30 minutes; then drain and squeeze out excess water.

❧ *Courtesy of Hill Country Cellars.*
 Serve with Hill Country Cellars Sauvignon Blanc.

WALNUT CREEK CE
VINTAGE
1984
TEXAS PORT
LIMITED BOTTLING
WIMBERLEY VALL
Messina Hop
PRIVATE RESERVE
PHEASANT RIDGE
Special Reserve
Frederick Thomas
Hill Country Cellars
Meats
AUGHTER LEFTWICH
VINEYARDS
AP ROCK
1994
CABERNET ROYALE
ROSÉ OF CABERNET SAUVIGNON
TEXAS
ALC 11% BY VOL
FALL CREEK
VINEYARDS
Grape
VINEY
ELL MOUNTAIN
ESTATE BOTTLED
STE. GENEVIEVE

Addison/James Vineyards Harvest Party Pork Loin

6–7 POUND PORK LOIN, PREPARED BY CUTTING OFF AS MUCH FAT AS POSSIBLE

Serves 6–8

Marinade

¼ CUP OLIVE OIL

2 LARGE TEXAS 1015 YELLOW ONIONS, SLICED

4 CARROTS, CLEANED, NOT PEELED, BUT SLICED

2 BAY LEAVES CRUSHED

½ TEASPOON DRIED THYME

¼ CUP COARSELY CHOPPED FRESH BASIL

1 WHOLE BULB GARLIC

1½ CUPS LA BUENA VIDA'S SPRINGTOWN RAIN OR LLANO ESTACADO SIGNATURE WHITE

1½ CUPS BOILING CHICKEN BROTH

4 WHOLE CLOVES

¼ TEASPOON CINNAMON

SALT AND PEPPER, TO TASTE

Sauté the onions, carrots, bay leaf, thyme, basil, and garlic in olive oil on medium heat until the onions are translucent. Add one cup wine, boiling chicken broth, cloves, and cinnamon; add salt and pepper to taste. Cover and simmer for 50–60 minutes. Strain, reserving the garlic bulb, and cool to baby's touch. Pour over pork loin in roasting pan, add marinade, cover, and refrigerate for at least 8–12 hours, and up to 24 hours, if possible.

Heat the oven to 350°.

Take the pork out of the marinade and place in a roasting pan with ½ cup of same marinade and ½ cup of same white wine. Cover and roast in oven for 2½ hours. Remove cover and roast for an additional 1½ hours, basting every half hour. Add more wine and marinade if necessary to keep the meat from burning.

Sauce

1	OUNCE BUTTER
2	LEEKS, CLEANED AND CHOPPED, WITH ABOUT TWO INCHES OF THE GREEN TOP
½	CUP OF SAME WHITE WINE
4	TABLESPOONS CORN STARCH
2	WHOLE SPRIGS OF FRESH CILANTRO
1 ½	CUPS OF BEEF STOCK
1	CHOPPED BAY LEAF
4	FRESH SAGE LEAVES, CHOPPED
½	TEASPOON FRESH CHOPPED ROSEMARY
5	JUNIPER BERRIES
	PULP FROM THE LEFTOVER COOKED MARINADE GARLIC
	SALT AND PEPPER, TO TASTE

Add the leeks, cilantro, and garlic pulp to melted butter in saucepan. Cook for 6 minutes over medium heat. Add the remaining ingredients plus two cups of leftover marinade. Simmer for ½ hour covered and ½ hour uncovered.

Remove the cooked pork from the roasting pan and place on a clean cutting board. Pour off any fat from the pan. Deglaze the pan with ½ cup of white wine. Pour the sauce through a strainer into the deglazed pan. Bring to a low, slow boil, and add corn starch diluted in ¾ cup of water. Add salt and pepper to taste.

Slice the pork ¾″ to 1″ thick. Place on a serving platter and pour sauce to thoroughly cover meat—roasted pork loin can be very dry—and provide a ½″ cover on bottom of platter. Reserve rest of marinade for potatoes or rice.

This is great when accompanied by oven-roasted, glazed potatoes, fresh sautéed mushrooms, and steamed whole carrots and parsnips.

❀ Contributed by Michael Zerbach, Texas Wine and Grape Growers Association, 1995 president.
*Serve with Hill Country Cellar's Barrel Reserve Chardonnay, La Buena Vida's Sauvignon Blanc, or Cap*Rock's Merlot.*

Beef on Croutons with Cabernet Mushroom Sauce and Walnut Salad

4   PIECES BEEF TENDERLOIN, 4 OUNCES EACH

½   TEASPOON SALT

2   TABLESPOONS OLIVE OIL

4   BREAD SLICES, ¼ INCH THICK

1   TABLESPOON BUTTER, UNSALTED

Sauce

1   TEASPOON OLIVE OIL

2   SHALLOTS, DICED

4   OUNCES MUSHROOMS (OYSTERS AND CRIMINIS)

1   TEASPOON GUAJILLO OR CHILI POWDER

¾   CUP FALL CREEK VINEYARDS CABERNET SAUVIGNON

1   CUP HEAVY WHIPPING CREAM

2   TABLESPOONS BASIL, CHOPPED

⅛   TEASPOON SEA SALT

Season beef with ⅛ teaspoon salt. In saucepan at medium heat, sear beef with olive oil for 1 minute each side; remove meat and set aside on a plate. In same pan, add 1 tablespoon butter and cook bread until light brown on both sides; remove bread from pan and raise the heat to high.

Add 1 teaspoon olive oil, shallots, and mushrooms; cook for 2 minutes. Deglaze with Cabernet and cook for 3 minutes until reduced by ⅓. Add cream and guajillo powder; cook another 3 minutes. Add basil and salt. Put beef over crouton, spoon sauce over it, and garnish with walnut salad (recipe follows).

Salad and Vinaigrette

4	OUNCES FRESH MUSTARD GREENS
¼	CUP WALNUTS ROASTED IN WALNUT OIL, SPRINKLED WITH ½ TEASPOON BROWN SUGAR
2	TABLESPOONS WALNUT OIL
1	TEASPOON DIJON MUSTARD
	JUICE OF 1 LEMON
¼	TEASPOON SEA SALT
	CRACKED BLACK PEPPER, TO TASTE

Mix all the vinaigrette ingredients in a bowl. In another bowl, toss mustard greens with vinaigrette until lightly coated. Divide onto four plates.

❧ *Contributed by David Garrido, Jeffrey's Restaurant, Austin.*
Serve with Fall Creek Vineyards Cabernet Sauvignon.

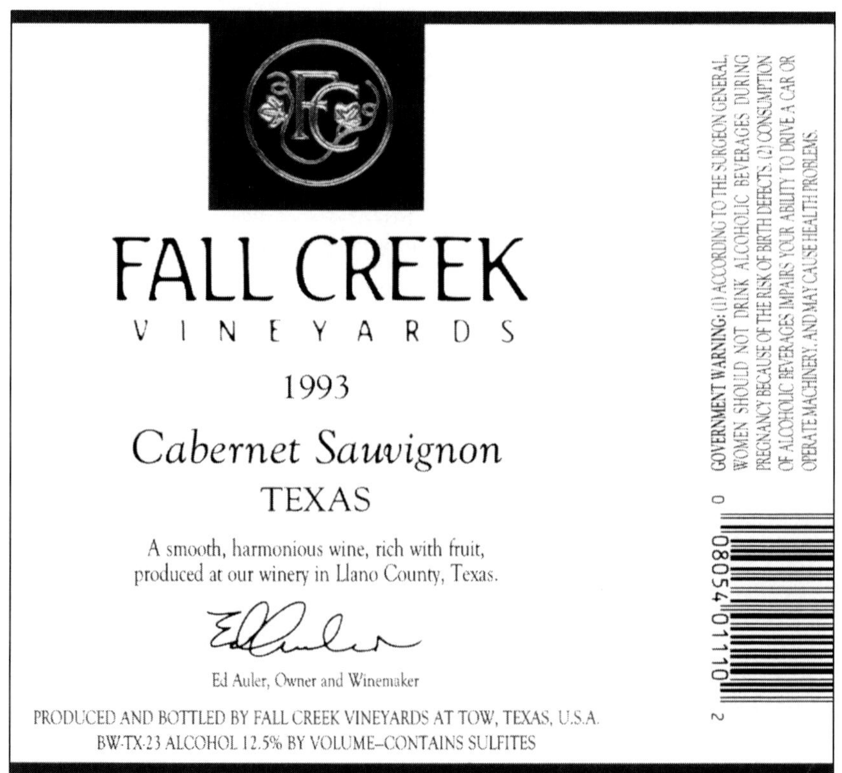

Beef Stew

Serves 6

- 2 POUNDS LEAN BONELESS BEEF CHUCK, CUT INTO ½″ PIECES
- 2 CUPS PHEASANT RIDGE CABERNET SAUVIGNON
- 2 LARGE ONIONS, CHOPPED
- 1 LARGE CARROT, CHOPPED
- 1 BAY LEAF
- 6 SPRIGS FRESH THYME (OR 1 TEASPOON DRIED)
- 2 GARLIC CLOVES, CHOPPED
- 7 SLICES BACON, CUT INTO ½″ PIECES
-    ALL-PURPOSE FLOUR
- 2 CUPS BEEF STOCK (OR CANNED BROTH)
- 2 LARGE TOMATOES, CHOPPED AND SEEDED

Combine first 7 ingredients in large bowl. Cover and refrigerate overnight. Remove beef from marinade and pat dry. Reserve marinade.

Cook bacon in heavy, large Dutch oven over high heat until brown. Transfer bacon to paper towel and drain well. Season beef with salt and pepper; coat with flour. Working in batches, add beef to drippings in Dutch oven and brown on all sides, about 7 minutes per batch. Return all beef to pot after browning. Add stock, tomatoes, marinade, and bacon; bring to a boil. Reduce heat and simmer one hour, covered.

Uncover pan and simmer until meat is tender and sauce thickens, about 1 hour and 15 minutes. Discard bay leaf. Season to taste with salt and pepper.

Stew may be served over noodles or as is.

❧ *Courtesy of William Gipson, Sr., owner, Pheasant Ridge Winery. Serve with Pheasant Ridge Cabernet Sauvignon.*

Beef Stew with Dried Cranberries

Serves 6

2	POUNDS BEEF (STEW MEAT, BONELESS CHUCK) OR VENISON
3	TABLESPOONS OLIVE OIL, DIVIDED
2	ONIONS, COARSELY CHOPPED
2	CLOVES GARLIC, MINCED
½	TEASPOON GROUND ALLSPICE
1	TEASPOON CRUMBLED, DRIED ROSEMARY
3	TABLESPOONS FLOUR
1	CUP DRIED CRANBERRIES
2	TABLESPOONS BALSAMIC VINEGAR
1	CUP BEEF BROTH
¾	CUP Pheasant Ridge Merlot, DIVIDED
1	TABLESPOON BROWN SUGAR
	SALT AND PEPPER, TO TASTE

Heat 1 tablespoon oil in Dutch oven over moderately high heat. Brown beef in batches, adding more oil as needed. Remove all beef from pan and set aside. Pour off fat.

Reduce heat to low, add 1 tablespoon oil to pan, then add onions and garlic. Cook for 3–5 minutes until softened.

Mix spices, flour, and cranberries together. Return beef to pan, add flour mixture, and stir well. Add vinegar, broth, and ½ cup wine. Stir well so that flour mixture is smoothly blended into liquid. Cook covered over low heat for about 2 hours, or until beef is tender. Stir occasionally.

Add additional wine to adjust consistency. Add brown sugar, salt and pepper to taste, and let simmer for 15 minutes.

Serve over freshly cooked noodles or Texas rice.

❧ Courtesy of Lois Sutton, Wines of America, Houston.
Serve with Pheasant Ridge Merlot.

Beef Stew with Red Wine

Serves 6

2	POUNDS LEAN BEEF CUT UP FOR STEW
¼	CUP FLOUR
2	TEASPOONS SALT
2	TABLESPOONS PURE VEGETABLE OR OLIVE OIL
1	8-OUNCE CAN TOMATO SAUCE
1	CUP HOT WATER
1	CUP PINEY WOODS COUNTRY WINES HEART OF TEXAS NOBLE RED MUSCADINE
¼	TEASPOON PEPPER
½	BAY LEAF
¼	TEASPOON THYME
6	EACH: SMALL POTATOES, CARROTS, SMALL ONIONS, ALL PEELED
2	BOUILLON CUBES
1	GREEN BELL PEPPER
1	CUP SLICED CELERY

Roll meat in flour mixed with salt. Brown slowly in hot oil in heavy kettle or pot. Add tomato sauce, water, wine, seasonings. Cover tightly, simmer about 1½ hours. Cut carrots, onions, potatoes, in quarters; bell peppers in eighths. Add to stew along with celery. Cover; simmer about 45 minutes longer.

Courtesy of Alfred Flies, Piney Woods Country Wines.
Serve with Piney Woods Country Wines Heart of Texas Noble Red Muscadine.

Beef Tenderloin with Tomato Cilantro Stuffing

"Angus beef is raised on the Fall Creek Ranch and is a big part of life at Fall Creek. This recipe is a delightful accompaniment with almost all beef dishes."—Susan Auler, co-owner, Fall Creek Vineyards.

Serves 8

1   BEEF TENDERLOIN (3½–4 POUNDS, FREE OF FAT AND SINEW), ROOM TEMPERATURE

½   CUP OLIVE OIL

2   TABLESPOONS BALSAMIC VINEGAR

Tomato Cilantro Stuffing, recipe follows

Whisk oil and vinegar together and pour over tenderloin. Marinate for 1–2 hours.

Pour off marinade and cut a deep slit in the center down the length of the tenderloin. Salt and pepper tenderloin. Stuff the slit or pocket with the tomato cilantro mixture.

Place stuffed tenderloin, uncovered, on a rack in roasting pan. Roast at 400° approximately 35 minutes for medium rare.

Tomato Cilantro Stuffing

3   TEASPOONS GARLIC, MINCED

1   TABLESPOON UNSALTED BUTTER

6   TABLESPOONS TOMATO PASTE

4   TABLESPOONS CHICKEN BROTH

½   TEASPOON SALT

4   TABLESPOONS CILANTRO, MINCED

1. Saute garlic in butter.
2. Add tomato paste, broth, and salt to garlic butter and cook until thick.
3. Remove from heat and stir in cilantro.

Serve with Fall Creek Vineyards Granite Reserve.

Boeuf Bourguignon

Serves 6

3	POUNDS STEWING MEAT (CHUCK), CUT INTO 2″ PIECES
½	CUP OIL
½	CUP MESSINA HOF GAMAY BEAUJOLAIS
1	CUP FLOUR
	SALT AND PEPPER, TO TASTE

Place all ingredients in a pot, bring to a boil and then let cool.

Marinade

3	CUPS MESSINA HOF GAMAY BEAUJOLAIS
1	SMALL ONION, SLICED
1	CARROT, SLICED
1	STALK CELERY
2	CLOVES GARLIC, CRUSHED
1	BAY LEAF
6	BLACK PEPPERCORNS, CRUSHED
½	CUP OIL

Arrange the meat cubes in a glass bowl; cover with the marinade. Refrigerate the meat for 10–12 hours, stirring 3–4 times.

Garnish

8   OUNCES BACON, CUT INTO SMALL STRIPS

25   PEARL ONIONS, COOKED, CANNED, OR FRESH

1   POUND FRESH MUSHROOMS, SLICED

1   TABLESPOON FRESH PARSLEY, CHOPPED

Remove the meat from the marinade, place on a cookie sheet or parchment paper. Dry the pieces of meat thoroughly with paper towels, then dust generously with flour.

In a heavy-based frying pan, cook the meat, a few pieces at a time, until brown.

Place the meat cubes in a Dutch oven or flameproof casserole dish. Strain vegetables from the marinade and sauté in the same fat. Add a little flour and cook over low heat, stirring continuously until the vegetables are light brown. Add the marinade, bring to a boil and simmer for 10 minutes.

Ladle the sauce over the meat cubes, cover the casserole and cook at low heat 325° for 3–4 hours, stirring occasionally.

When the meat is tender, remove from sauce with a slotted spoon and transfer to serving dish.

In the meantime, sauté the bacon in a medium frying pan; add the onions and mushrooms. Discard any excess fat and strain the sauce over the garnish and bring to a boil. Taste for seasoning if necessary. Pour the sauce over the Beef Bourguignon, sprinkle with freshly chopped parsley, and serve with noodles or boiled potatoes.

❧ Courtesy of Joe Mannke, owner and chef, Rotisserie for Beef and Bird, Houston. Serve with Llano Estacado Cabernet Sauvignon.

Bell Mountain Roast Beef of Tenderloin

Serves 8

3–5   POUND BEEF TENDERLOIN, EXCESS FAT AND TIP END REMOVED

Marinade

BELL MOUNTAIN CABERNET SAUVIGNON, TO COVER

1   PEELED SHALLOT BULB, CHOPPED

2   TABLESPOONS FRESH THYME LEAVES (REMOVED FROM STEMS, BUT NOT CHOPPED)

¼   FRESH LEMON, CHOPPED, PEEL INCLUDED

Marinate beef for 16–24 hours in a narrow, deep glass casserole dish.

Turn beef about every 6–8 hours.

After marinating, drain marinade from casserole into a saucepan and reserve.

Place tenderloin back into baking casserole dish, which has been greased with butter or sprayed with non-stick cooking spray.

Spread soft butter over top of tenderloin and then pat on:

3   TABLESPOONS FRESH THYME LEAVES

3   PEELED SHALLOT BULBS, CHOPPED

¼   FRESH LEMON, CHOPPED, PEEL INCLUDED

Sprinkle over top of tenderloin:

COARSE GROUND BLACK PEPPER

SEA SALT

Preheat oven to 500° and sear tenderloin in casserole dish for 5 minutes per pound. Reduce heat to 225° and bake 20 to 30 minutes per pound, depending on desired doneness.

Heat marinade in saucepan to boil, and reduce by about one half. Blend 4 tablespoons butter into 2 tablespoons flour and stir into marinade; continue to stir constantly until sauce thickens.

Garnish carving platter with parsley. Carve into ½-inch slices.

Courtesy of Bob Oberhelman, owner and winemaker, Bell Mountain Vineyards.
Serve with Bell Mountain Cabernet Sauvignon.

Butterflied Leg of Lamb

1	LEG OF LAMB
1	TABLESPOON SOY SAUCE
	JUICE OF ½ LEMON
1	TEASPOON GROUND ROSEMARY
1	TEASPOON GROUND MINT
1	CLOVE GARLIC, MINCED

Purchase lamb butterflied. Trim any excess fat or membrane and score in 2 or 3 places, 1½″ cuts. Mix together soy sauce, lemon juice, rosemary, ground mint, and garlic. Marinate lamb in mixture in refrigerator for 4 hours.

Grill over hot fire for 35–45 minutes to desired degree of doneness. Let sit 8 minutes prior to carving. Carve in ¼″ slices. Serve without a sauce.

Courtesy of Mary Cook, Wines of America, Houston.
Serve with Pheasant Ridge Proprietor's Reserve Red.

Carpetbagger Steak

Serves 4

4	CENTER-CUT TENDERLOIN STEAKS, 2″ THICK
8	RAW OYSTERS
2	TABLESPOONS OLIVE OIL
2	TABLESPOONS UNSALTED BUTTER
	SALT AND PEPPER

Make a pocket in each steak by cutting a slit deep into the side. Tuck 2 oysters into each steak and skewer the pockets shut with toothpicks.

In a large skillet, heat olive oil and butter over high heat until almost smoking. Add the steaks and brown all over, including the edges, about 1 minute. Reduce heat to low and cook the steaks 5 minutes on each side for medium rare. Season with salt and pepper to taste.

May be served with a Béarnaise sauce, if desired.

Courtesy of Hill Country Cellars.
Serve with Hill Country Cellars Cabernet Sauvignon.

Cassoulet Santa Fe French Pork and Beans with a Southwestern Flair

Serves
10–12

"For do-ahead holiday fare, put this hearty bean-and-meat dish together before the festivities begin. It freezes well, has a barrage of flavors, and, with the combination of pork, lamb, and chicken (or duck), feeds a crowd. Serve with cornbread and a tray of assorted vegetables."—Shirley Jones, Southwest editor *Ameri   Wine on the Web.*

Beans

    4   CUPS DRY WHITE BEANS, SUCH AS NAVY OR GREAT
         NORTHERN
    4   QUARTS WATER OR CHICKEN STOCK
    2   MEDIUM-SIZE ONIONS, QUARTERED
    3   GARLIC CLOVES, FINELY CHOPPED
    1   DRIED RED ANCHO CHILI POD, SEEDS REMOVED
  3–4   CELERY TOPS
    1   TEASPOON CORIANDER

Soak the beans overnight or, if you wish, use a pressure cooker. Simply place beans and the remaining ingredients in pot and cook, over low heat, until beans are done. Depending on your altitude, this may take two to four hours. If using a pressure cooker, follow time suggestion for dried beans.

Meats

  4–6   PIECES COOKED CHICKEN OR DUCK
    ½   POUND CHORIZO OR OTHER SAUSAGE
  4–6   LAMB CHOPS
    1   POUND PORK TENDERLOIN, CUT IN 2″ PIECES
  4–5   SLICES BACON, CUT INTO 1″ PIECES
    1   MEDIUM ONION, CHOPPED
    2   GARLIC CLOVES, FINELY CHOPPED
    1   TEASPOON CORIANDER
    1   TABLESPOON CUMIN
    1   CUP LLANO ESTACADO SIGNATURE WHITE
    1   BAY LEAF
         SALT, TO TASTE

Grill, smoke, or roast chicken (or duck).
For the lamb and pork, fry the bacon in large skillet. Remove bacon and set aside. In about 1 tablespoon of bacon drippings, sauté onions until

transparent. Add garlic, lamb, and pork. Brown the meats over medium heat. Reduce heat. Add wine, cumin, coriander, salt, and bay leaf. Cover and cook until done. Remove bay leaf.

Fry chorizo according to package directions, or simply fry in a lightly greased skillet. Slice into ½″ pieces, if possible. Some links simply break apart. Beware: some manufacturers use a non-edible casing, so read the label.

Topping

1–1 ½   CUPS BREAD CRUMBS

Preheat oven to 350°.

Drain the beans, salt them if you wish, but reserve liquid. Place about a 1″ layer of beans in a heavy, flameproof 6–8 quart casserole. Place some of the lamb-pork mixture over the beans, along with 2 or 3 pieces of chicken, some chorizo, and bacon. Continue layering until casserole is filled with beans as last layer. Pour bean liquid into casserole until mixture is covered. (Optional: add about ¼ cup sherry at this point.) Top the dish with bread crumbs. Bake for 1–2 hours.

*Note: You can freeze the cassoulet before or after baking. Defrost before heating. Serve with Cap*Rock Cabernet Royale or Cap*Rock Brut Sparkling Wine.*

Chuck Wagon Chili

Serves 10–12

1	POUND PINTO BEANS
3	POUNDS LEAN ROUND STEAK, CUT INTO 1″ CUBES
1	CUP TEXAS CABERNET SAUVIGNON
1	15-OUNCE CAN TOMATO SAUCE
1	6-OUNCE CAN TOMATO PASTE
1	4½-OUNCE CAN CHOPPED GREEN CHILES
5¼	TEASPOONS CHILI POWDER
2¼	TEASPOONS OREGANO
1½	TEASPOONS CUMIN
1½	TEASPOONS SALT
1½	TEASPOONS CAYENNE PEPPER
1½	TEASPOONS RED HOT SAUCE
	WATER
¼	CUP FLOUR (OPTIONAL)

Rinse pinto beans; follow package directions for quick soak method. After soaking beans for one hour, drain beans and thoroughly rinse. Set aside.

Cook lean beef in wine until brown. Add pinto beans and stir in tomato sauce, tomato paste, chopped green chiles, chili powder, oregano, cumin, salt, cayenne pepper, and hot sauce.

Add water to cover 1″ above meat mixture. Simmer 2 hours or until meat and beans are tender. Skim off fat. If a thicker liquid is desired, combine about ¼ cup flour and enough water to make a paste. Add a small amount of hot liquid to flour mixture; stir. Pour into chili and stir to combine. Cook until mixture has thickened.

Chuck Wagon Chili is better when refrigerated overnight and reheated before serving.

❧ *Courtesy of Rick Perry, Commissioner, Texas Department of Agriculture. Serve with Texas Chenin Blanc.*

Coffee-roasted Fillet of Beef with Sage and Wild Mushrooms (with Cheddar Cheese Grits)

Coffee-roasted Fillet of Beef

Serves 4–6

2	POUNDS FILLET OF BEEF, CENTER CUT, HELD TOGETHER WITH STRING
2	TABLESPOONS VIRGIN OLIVE OIL
1	TEASPOON COARSE SALT
1	TEASPOON FRESHLY GROUND BLACK PEPPER
1	TABLESPOON FINELY MINCED FRESH SAGE
2	TABLESPOONS FINELY GROUND COFFEE BEANS
1	TABLESPOON COCOA POWDER

Cheddar Cheese Grits

3½	CUPS WATER
1½	TEASPOONS SALT
1	CUP WHITE GRITS
¼	CUP HEAVY CREAM
8	OUNCES SHARP CHEDDAR CHEESE

Wild Mushrooms

    2   TABLESPOONS BUTTER

    ½   WHITE ONION, MINCED

    4   CLOVES GARLIC, MINCED

    1   POUND WILD MUSHROOMS (SHIITAKE), STEMS REMOVED
    AND DISCARDED, MUSHROOMS CAPS ROUGHLY
    CHOPPED

    1   TABLESPOON FINELY CHOPPED FRESH SAGE

    1   TEASPOON COARSE SALT

    ½   TEASPOON BLACK PEPPER

Garnishes

    2   TABLESPOONS VIRGIN OLIVE OIL

        SAGE LEAVES SAUTÉED IN BUTTER

Rub the fillet with the olive oil. Combine the salt, pepper, coffee, and cocoa powder. Spread the mixture over a work surface and roll the fillet in the mixture to evenly coat the beef. Allow to marinate approximately 30 minutes.

Preheat an oven to 400°. Place the fillet on a rack in a roasting pan. Put the fillet in the oven and immediately lower the heat to 250°. After 20 minutes, check the internal temperature of the fillet (125° for medium-rare or 135° for medium). If more cooking is necessary, return the beef to the oven (still set at 250°) and slowly roast to the desired temperature. Remove the fillet from the oven and allow to rest (uncovered) in a warm place for about five minutes before carving. Before carving, remove the string.

While the fillet is roasting, prepare the grits. In a 2-quart sauce pan, heat the water and salt to a boil. Stir in the grits. Lower the heat to a simmer. Stir frequently until thick. If the grits become too thick, add additional water. Keep covered and warm. Just before serving, add the cream and the grated cheddar cheese. Stir until the cheese melts.

Just before carving the fillet of beef, sauté the wild mushrooms. Heat a large skillet over medium-high heat. Add the butter and sauté the onion and garlic until lightly browned. Add the mushrooms and sage, and sauté slowly until lightly browned. Continually turn and stir the mushrooms allowing the juices in the pan to nicely caramelize (but do not burn). Add salt and pepper to taste.

To serve, place a spoonful of cheddar cheese grits in the center of each plate. Thinly slice the fillet and arrange over the grits. Spoon the mushrooms over the slices of fillet. Drizzle a little virgin olive oil over the beef and arrange some sautéed sage leaves over the beef.

*❧ Courtesy of Robert del Grande, Café Annie, Houston.
Serve with Fall Creek Vineyards Granite Reserve.*

Country-baked Ham with Chardonnay Mustard Glaze

Serves 8

1	5-POUND HAM
2	TABLESPOONS GINGER
½	CUP MESSINA HOF CHARDONNAY MUSTARD (OR ANY WHITE WINE MUSTARD, NOT DIJON)
¼	CUP MESSINA HOF CHARDONNAY

Insert ginger pieces under skin of ham. Coat ham with mixture of other two ingredients and bake until tender, approximately 20 minutes per pound. (Make sure internal temperature is 160°.) Baste every 20 minutes until done.

*❧ Courtesy of Messina Hof Wine Cellars.
Serve with Messina Hof White Zinfandel.*

Flank Steak with Tomato-Olive Sauce

Serves 4

1½   POUNDS FLANK STEAK, TRIMMED, AT ROOM
        TEMPERATURE

8   CANNED ITALIAN PLUM TOMATOES, SEEDED, COARSELY
        CHOPPED, AND DRAINED WELL

1   SMALL CLOVE GARLIC, MASHED

8   OIL-CURED OLIVES, HALVED, PITTED, AND CUT INTO
        THIN STRIPS

1   LARGE SHALLOT, FINELY DICED

1   TEASPOON WHITE WINE VINEGAR

3   TABLESPOONS EXTRA VIRGIN OLIVE OIL

½   TEASPOON COARSELY GROUND PEPPER

      SALT

2   TABLESPOONS FINELY CHOPPED PARSLEY

In a pan that will hold all the steak comfortably, heat enough water to cover, about a ½ inch, to 140°.

Add the steak. Poach for 7 minutes. Turn steak over and poach 7–8 minutes longer, until rare. The steak is rare when it is springy to the touch in the center and the internal temperature is 135°–140°.

Remove steak to a platter, cover loosely, and let cool to room temperature. Then slice and serve, or wrap well and refrigerate overnight.

Sauce

In a medium bowl, combine the tomatoes, garlic, olives, shallot, vinegar, oil, pepper, and salt. Let stand for 1 hour or overnight, to let the flavors blend. Just before serving, stir in parsley.

To serve, slice the steak very thin on the diagonal for maximum tenderness. Spoon sauce over meat.

Courtesy of Hill Country Cellars.
Serve with Hill Country Cellars Merlot.

French Meat Pie

"My mother made this pie every Christmas Eve. She made it when I was a little girl. We are Canadian French, and it's one of my favorites."—Rita Zerbach, mother of Michael Zerbach, president of the Texas Wine and Grape Growers Association

Serves 6–8

2	TABLESPOONS COOKING OIL
1	LARGE ONION SLICED
1	POUND GROUND BEEF
1	POUND GROUND PORK
1	CUP MASHED POTATOES
1	TEASPOON SALT
¼	TEASPOON PEPPER
	PASTRY FOR DOUBLE-CRUST PIE, 9 INCHES
1	EGG, BEATEN

In a skillet, heat oil over medium heat. Sauté onion until tender. Remove and set aside. Brown beef and pork together in same skillet, then drain. Combine onion, meat, potatoes, and seasoning.

Line pie plate with pastry. Fill with meat mixture and top with crust. Brush with egg if desired. Bake at 375° for 30–35 minutes, or until golden brown. Serve plain or with your favorite sour cream gravy.

Serve with La Buena Vida Sauvignon Blanc.

Good Pork Chops

"My mother used to make this when I lived at home, and it was one of my favorite dishes. I took this recipe to college, and won over my boyfriend, now husband, with this one."—Lisa Rydman Elder, Spec's Liquor Store, Houston.

4	PORK CHOPS
1	10¾-OUNCE CAN CREAM OF CELERY SOUP
1	PINT SOUR CREAM
	HICKORY SALT, TO TASTE

1. Brown chops and place in baking dish.
2. Mix together soup, sour cream, and salt. Pour over chops.
3. Bake at 350° for 45 minutes.
4. Serve with rice.

❧ *Serve with Messina Hof Gamay Beaujolais.*

Grilled Veal Medallion with Ancho Chili Potato and Red Pepper Aioli

---

Ancho Chili Potato

Serves 6

4   LARGE IDAHO POTATOES

1   TABLESPOON GROUND ANCHO CHILI

⅓   CUP HEAVY WHIPPING CREAM

    SALT AND PEPPER

    OIL FOR DEEP FRYING

⅓   CUP JULIENNED CARROTS

⅓   CUP JULIENNED RUTABAGA

Shred one potato on a mandoline to make large gaufrette potatoes. Fry them for 10 seconds in deep fryer until soft. Line 2½″ circle molds with parchment paper, place 3 slices of gaufrette potato in molds, bake until brown, and take out. Make the mashed potato and mix in the ground Ancho chile, cream, salt, and pepper.

Red Pepper Aioli

2   RED PEPPERS ROASTED, PEELED, AND CLEANED

2   EGG YOLKS

1   CUP OLIVE OIL

1   TEASPOON DIJON MUSTARD

1   TABLESPOON BALSAMIC VINEGAR

In a blender add egg yolk, mustard, and red pepper. While the motor is running, pour in one cup of olive oil in a slow stream, until the mixture is emulsified; then add the balsamic vinegar.

12	2½-OUNCE VEAL MEDALLIONS
1	POUND FRESH SPINACH

Grill veal medallion over charcoal until medium rare.

Pipe the Ancho mashed potato into the crisp potato circle. Wilt the spinach by sautéeing in butter and arrange on bottom. Layer with sautéed carrots and rutabaga. Top with 2 veal medallions. Streak the plate with Red Pepper Aioli.

Courtesy of Clive O'Donoghue, Director of Food and Beverage, Four Seasons Resort and Club, Las Colinas, Dallas. Serve with Fall Creek Semillon-Sauvignon Blanc.

Ham Steaks Sautéed in Red Wine

1½	POUNDS COOKED HAM, SLICED ⅜″ THICK	Serves 4
2	TABLESPOONS UNSALTED BUTTER	
1	TABLESPOON LIGHT OLIVE OIL	
2	TABLESPOONS MINCED SHALLOTS OR SCALLIONS	
⅓	CUP GRAPE CREEK CABERNET TROIS	
⅓	CUP HAM OR BEEF STOCK	

Use a frying pan large enough to hold the ham steaks comfortably and use a cover. Trim off excess fat and cut into serving size pieces; pat dry with paper towels. Heat butter and oil in frying pan; after foaming subsides, brown ham steaks on both sides for a minute or two.

Add shallots, wine, and stock. Cover and simmer for 5 minutes. Remove ham to a hot plate, boil juices down to a syrup, spoon over ham, and serve with buttered spinach and mashed potatoes.

❧ Courtesy of Ned and Nell Simes, owners, Grape Creek Vineyard, Stonewall. Serve with Grape Creek Cabernet Trois or Grape Creek Chardonnay.

Herb-crusted Lamb with Maple Au Jus

Serves 2

10	OUNCES LAMB LOIN, CLEANED
2	TABLESPOONS MESSINA HOF CHARDONNAY
3	OUNCES DIJON MUSTARD
1	OUNCE WHITE WORCESTERSHIRE SAUCE
1	OUNCE FRESH BASIL, CHOPPED
1	OUNCE THYME
1	OUNCE RED AND GREEN BELL PEPPERS, FLAKED
1	OUNCE CHIVES
	SALT AND PEPPER, TO TASTE
2	OUNCES AU JUS GRAVY OR BEEF STOCK
1	OUNCE MAPLE SYRUP
1	OUNCE LIME JUICE

Mix Messina Hof Chardonnay with Dijon mustard and white Worcestershire sauce. In separate pan mix basil, thyme, red and green bell pepper flakes, and chives. Coat one side of lamb with mustard mix and then with herb mix. Bake in medium oven, or sauté lamb until medium rare. Heat sauce for 2–3 minutes, stirring well. Slice lamb into ¼″ slices and drizzle with sauce.

❧ Courtesy of Charles Watkins, owner and chef, Sierra Grill, Houston. Serve with Messina Hof Private Reserve Cabernet Sauvignon.

Lone Star Scaloppini Suprema

Serves 6–8

¼	CUP EXTRA VIRGIN OLIVE OIL
1	CUP CHOPPED ONION
1	LARGE GARLIC CLOVE, MINCED
1	CUP CHOPPED GREEN PEPPER
½	CUP CHOPPED PARSLEY
2	BAY LEAVES
1	16–OUNCE CAN TOMATOES, UNDRAINED AND CHOPPED
1	CUP TOMATO JUICE
1	6–OUNCE CAN TOMATO PASTE
1	4½–OUNCE JAR MUSHROOMS
1	CUP HOT WATER
1	TABLESPOON SALT
1	TEASPOON PEPPER
¼	CUP MESSINA HOF "ANGEL" JOHANNISBERG RIESLING
2	POUNDS THIN VEAL SCALLOPS (ABOUT 14 PIECES)
	COOKED RICE

Heat cup oil in large saucepan. Add garlic and onion; sauté until tender. Stir in green pepper, parsley, and bay leaves. Cook, uncovered, over low heat until tender, about 5 minutes, stirring several times. Blend in tomatoes, juice, tomato paste, and mushrooms. Add water and simmer uncovered 30 minutes. Stir in seasonings and cook 15 minutes more, stirring occasionally. Remove bay leaves.

Preheat oven to 350°. Stir wine into sauce. In large skillet, heat small amount of oil. Sauté veal scallops in batches 1–2 minutes on each side. Drain on paper towels. Place scallops in 9″ × 13″ baking dish. Pour sauce over meat. Cover and cook 30 minutes. Serve over rice. May be prepared in advance and reheated.

❋ *Courtesy of Stu Burge, Executive Director, Texas Wine and Grape Growers Association, Colleyville.*
Serve with Messina Hof Gamay Beaujolais.

Marinated Flank Steak

1½	POUNDS FLANK STEAK
¼	CUP OLIVE OIL
⅛	CUP SOY SAUCE
2	TABLESPOONS MALT VINEGAR
2	TABLESPOONS KETCHUP
2–4	CLOVES GARLIC, CHOPPED

Combine all ingredients in food processor and blend until smooth. Marinate the flank steak for 8–12 hours. Grill on a hot grill until cooked medium. The outside should be brown and the inside should have just a hint of pink left. You can also soak 8 ounces sliced mushrooms in the same marinade and sauté them for a delicious accompaniment.

Courtesy of Linda Metzler, Wines of America, Houston.
*Serve with Cap*Rock Reserve Cabernet Sauvignon.*

Prime Ribs

    3   POUNDS RIB ROAST

    1   TEASPOON PAPRIKA

    2   GARLIC CLOVES, CRUSHED

    1¼   CUPS GRAPE CREEK CABERNET TROIS

    1¼   CUPS RED WINE VINEGAR

Rub herbed olive oil and garlic onto meat. Sprinkle with paprika. Marinate in red wine and vinegar for approximately 4–6 hours. Roast on a rack until desired degree of doneness. Serve with baked potatoes, sour cream, and a horseradish sauce.

❀ *Courtesy of Ned and Nell Simes, owners, Grape Creek Vineyard, Stonewall. Serve with Grape Creek Cabernet Trois.*

Roast Rack of Lamb

    2   RACKS TEXAS SPRING LAMB, TRIMMED (ABOUT

         1½ POUNDS EACH)

    1   TEASPOON THYME

         SALT AND PEPPER

    1   TEASPOON VEGETABLE OIL

    ½   CUP HILL COUNTRY CELLARS CABERNET SAUVIGNON

Preheat oven to 450°. Season the lamb with thyme, salt, and pepper. Place in roasting pan and sprinkle with oil.

Roast for 30–40 minutes, according to taste. (Rack of lamb is best when quite pink.)

Transfer the roasted lamb to a serving platter. Discard all but 1 table-spoon of the drippings from pan. Deglaze the pan with Hill Country Cellars Cabernet Sauvignon.

Pour the juices over the lamb and carve.

❦ Courtesy of Leigh Burns, Hill Country Cellars.
Serve with Hill Country Cellars Cabernet Sauvignon.

Texas Tartare

Serves 6–8

1	POUND BEEF TENDERLOIN
6	ANCHOVY FILLETS
3	EGG YOLKS
4½	TEASPOONS LA BUENA VIDA VINEYARDS WALNUT CREEK TEXAS PORT
¾	TEASPOON DIJON MUSTARD
½	TEASPOON WORCESTERSHIRE SAUCE
3	DROPS HOT PEPPER SAUCE
1½	TABLESPOONS MINCED ONION
1	TEASPOON DRAINED, MINCED CAPERS
½	TEASPOON MINCED SWEET BASIL
1	TEASPOON MINCED DILL PICKLE
1	TEASPOON MINCED FRESH PARSLEY
½	TEASPOON SPANISH PAPRIKA
¼	TEASPOON SALT
¼	TEASPOON FRESHLY GROUND PEPPER
	MINCED FRESH PARSLEY FOR GARNISH

Finely hand chop chilled beef. Mash anchovies in medium bowl. Add egg yolks, port, mustard, Worcestershire sauce, pepper sauce, and mix well. Stir in onion, capers, basil, pickle, parsley, and paprika. Add raw

beef, salt and pepper, and blend thoroughly. Transfer to a chilled serving
plate and garnish with minced parsley.

*❧ Courtesy of Stu Burge, Executive Director, Texas Wine and Grape Growers
Association, Colleyville.
Serve with Llano Estacado Cellar Select Cabernet Sauvignon.*

Veal Saltom Boca

Serves 6

12	SLICES VEAL, 3–4 OUNCES EACH
12	TABLESPOONS SAGE
	SALT, PEPPER
12	SLICES PROSCIUTTO HAM, THIN
12	SLICES PROVOLONE CHEESE, THIN
12	SLICES TOMATO, THIN
3	OUNCES OLIVE OIL
1	POUND MUSHROOMS, SLICED
½	CLOVE GARLIC FINELY CHOPPED
2	CUPS MESSINA HOF PAPA PAULO PORT WINE
3	TABLESPOONS BUTTER

Pound veal slices until thin. Distribute sage among the slices by rubbing
a little on each; salt and pepper each slice to taste. Then, stack the pro-
sciutto, cheese, and tomato, in order, on one side of each slice and roll
tightly. Secure the veal rolls with toothpicks.

In a large skillet, heat olive oil until hot. Dredge the veal rolls in flour, shaking off the excess, and place them in the skillet. Sauté both sides until gold-
en brown, adding the mushrooms and garlic when browning the second
side. Remove veal and keep warm. Add port and de-glaze the skillet, scraping up any bits from the skillet; discard garlic. Cover. Reduce port to half and

return the veal. Remove lid and add butter. Arrange veal on a platter, thicken sauce, and spread sauce on the veal. Serve immediately.

❧ *Courtesy of Messina Hof Wine Cellars.*
Serve with Messina Hof Gamay Beaujolais.

Veal Scaloppini with Mushroom Sauce

Serves 4

2	POUNDS BROWN MUSHROOMS, SLICED
½	CUP BUTTER
1	BOTTLE MESSINA HOF PAPA PAULO PORT
20	FRESH BASIL LEAVES
	OLIVE OIL
8	PIECES VEAL SCALLOPINI, 3–4 OUNCES EACH
1	CUP FLOUR
1	EGG
1	CUP SEASONED BREAD CRUMBS
	CURLED PEEL OF LEMON

Sauté sliced mushrooms in ½ cup butter. Gradually add wine as each addition is absorbed into mushrooms. After all wine is added, let simmer 1 hour over low heat with fresh basil. This sauce may be frozen for later use.

Just prior to serving, heat the olive oil in a skillet. Coat veal with flour, dip in egg, then dip in the seasoned bread crumbs. Cook veal on each side for two minutes on a hot skillet.

Put veal on a plate and top with the mushroom sauce. Garnish with lemon peel.

❧ *Courtesy of Messina Hof Wine Cellars.*
Serve with Messina Hof Cabernet Franc.

WALNUT CREEK CE
VINTAGE
1984
TEXAS PORT
LIMITED BOTTLING
WIMBERLEY VALLE
Messina Hof
PRIVATE RESERVE
HEASANT RIDGE
Special Reserve
Game
Hill Country Cellars
SLAUGHTER LEFTWICH
VINEYARDS
AP·ROCK
1994
CABERNET ROYALE
SÉ OF CABERNET SAUVIGNON
TEXAS
ALC 11% BY VOL
FALL CREEK
VINEYARDS
Grape
VINEY
LL MOUNTAIN
ESTATE BOTTLED
STE. GENEVIEVE
199
TEXA
CHARDO

Bacon-wrapped Smoked Venison Loin with Kiln-dried Cherry Sauce

"I first made this dish for my family reunion, although it was not the featured item. When I showed my cousins in Pennsylvania how to make Texas Barbecue, the pit was loaded with brisket I had brought up for the occasion. As the briskets were done, I took them into the house to refrigerate for the next day. Soon, about 20 relatives were involved in the family's annual poker game. When they smelled the brisket, their hunger got the better of them. The next thing I knew, all the brisket for the reunion was gone. Since you can't just run off and buy brisket in Pennsylvania, I asked my cousin for some fresh venison. This is the recipe I concocted; I hope you enjoy it as well as my entire family did." —David Schnell, Executive Chef, The Houston Club.

Serves 6 as dinner, or 12 as appetizer

2	POUNDS BONELESS VENISON LOIN
¾	POUND THICK-SLICED, CURED SMOKED BACON
¼	POUND CAUL FAT*
	SALT AND BLACK PEPPER TO TASTE

Season the loin with salt and pepper and sear in a hot skillet until golden brown. Let cool.

Spread out the caul fat, then lay out the bacon in one layer the length of the loin. Trim the bacon, so that when you roll it up, the bacon should overlap about ¼". Place venison on top of bacon and roll up with caul fat.

Smoke, preferably with hickory wood, for 1 hour at 190° or until internal temperature of venison is 125° (medium-rare to medium). Wait 10 minutes before slicing.

*This is the stomach fat layer, usually pork, that looks like fish netting. Ask your butcher for this product. It is primarily used to hold the roladen together and shape the final product. This fat itself will cook completely away.

Sauce

2	TABLESPOONS BUTTER
¼	CUP FINE DICED SHALLOTS
1	TABLESPOON MINCED GARLIC
2	CUPS KILN-DRIED CHERRIES
2	TABLESPOONS SUGAR
1	CUP PHEASANT RIDGE PROPRIETORS RESERVE CABERNET SAUVIGNON
1	CUP VAL VERDE DON LUIS TEXAS TAWNY PORT
3	CUPS DEMI-GLAZE BEEF STOCK
2	TEASPOONS SWEET BASIL
	SALT AND BLACK PEPPER TO TASTE

In butter, sauté shallots and garlic until tender. Add one cup of the cherries and sugar, and sauté for one minute. Add the red wine and port, bring to a simmer, and reduce by three quarters. Place into food processor and puree. Then, strain into sauce pot. Add remaining cherries and stock; simmer for 10 minutes. Add basil and season to taste.

❧ *Serve with Pheasant Ridge Merlot.*

Breast of Pheasant with Grapes and Pine Nuts

3	PHEASANTS, 2 POUNDS EACH
½	CUP OLIVE OIL
6	CLOVES GARLIC, PEELED AND CHOPPED
1	TABLESPOON SOY SAUCE
1	CUP HEAVY CREAM
2	10¾-OUNCE CANS MUSHROOM SOUP
8	OUNCES FRESH MUSHROOMS
8	OUNCES BUTTER
4	OUNCES FLOUR
4	OUNCES PINE NUTS
8	OUNCES GREEN GRAPES, HALVED
4	SHALLOTS OR ½ SMALL ONION
4	OUNCES DRY SHERRY

With a sharp knife, remove the two breasts from the center bone and all the meat from the legs.

Remove all the skin and excess fat, place the pheasant breasts and legs in a ceramic dish. Marinate with the garlic, soy sauce, and olive oil, overnight if possible.

Melt the butter in a heavy skillet, season the pheasants with salt and pepper, dip in flour, and sauté over low heat until light brown.

Remove the pheasants from the skillet and place on a heated platter. Add more butter to the pan if necessary, add the onions, and simmer. Combine with the fresh mushrooms, mushroom soup, sherry wine, heavy cream, grapes, and bring to a boil. Garnish with pine nuts and ladle over the pheasants; serve with fettuccine.

Courtesy of Joe Mannke, owner and chef, Rotisserie for Beef and Bird, Houston.
Serve with Hill Country Chardonnay, Special Reserve.

Delectable Dove

18   WHOLE OR BREASTED DOVES

      ALL-PURPOSE FLOUR

      SALT

¾   CUP BUTTER

      BACON GREASE

½   CUP CHOPPED ONION

1   8 OUNCE CAN CHOPPED MUSHROOMS, RESERVE JUICE

2   TEASPOONS CHOPPED PARSLEY

1   CUP HILL COUNTRY CELLARS SAUVIGNON BLANC

1   CUP WHIPPING CREAM

Rub mixture of flour and salt into doves. Sauté doves in butter and small amount of bacon grease.

Remove doves and place in greased baking dish, breast side down.

Sauté onion, mushrooms, and parsley in remaining butter. Add wine and mushroom juice. Pour over doves. Bake, covered, for 2 hours at 300°. Baste frequently. Add cream and bake an additional 30 minutes.

❧ *Courtesy of Hill Country Cellars.*
Serve with Hill Country Cellars Sauvignon Blanc.

Grilled Medallions of Venison with Wild Mushrooms and Blackberry Sage Sauce

Serves 6

2 TABLESPOONS FINELY MINCED FRESH SAGE

1 TABLESPOON FRESHLY GROUND BLACK PEPPER

1 TABLESPOON KOSHER SALT

1 TABLESPOON GARLIC SALT

1 3 POUND LOIN OF VENISON, CUT INTO 1" THICK MEDALLIONS

¼ CUP OLIVE OIL

Season venison medallions and sear in olive oil. Place on rack with pan and finish cooking in a 350° oven until medium-rare.

Blackberry Sage Sauce

¼ CUP OLIVE OIL

¼ CUP CHOPPED SHALLOTS

2½ CUPS VEAL STOCK

1 CUP Messina Hof Cabernet Sauvignon

1 CUP FRESH BLACKBERRIES

2 TABLESPOONS CHOPPED FRESH SAGE LEAVES

SALT AND FRESHLY GROUND PEPPER TO TASTE

Sauté shallots in olive oil until soft. Add stock and wine, and reduce to a light sauce consistency. Add blackberries and sage, and simmer for 20 minutes. Salt and pepper to taste.

Mushrooms

½   CUP SLICED SHIITAKE MUSHROOMS

½   CUP SLICED OYSTER MUSHROOMS

¼   CUP CHICKEN STOCK

Sauté all over high heat until soft and tender.

To serve, place 3 medallions on each plate, top with mushrooms, and drizzle sauce over all. Garnish with whole fresh blackberries and fresh sage sprigs.

❋ *Courtesy of Jimmy Mitchell, Executive Chef, Rainbow Lodge, Houston. Serve with Messina Hof Cabernet Sauvignon.*

Peppered Venison Loin with Currant Sauce

For more than a decade, the Houston Club has conducted the Best of Texas Wine Awards and Tasting, two events that identify and celebrate publicly the finest wines produced in the state. This venison dish was prepared by Executive Chef David Schnell for a Retrospective Dinner, featuring the Best of Texas medal winners from 1994, on September 14, 1995, at the Houston Club.

4 6-OUNCE PIECES VENISON LOIN

SALT AND FRESHLY GROUND BLACK PEPPER TO TASTE

Serves 4

Season the loins with salt and heavily with coarse ground pepper until evenly coated. Sear in hot skillet and roast in 350° oven until medium-rare. Slice in half on a bias and serve on a bed of red cabbage with currant sauce.

Red Cabbage

1½   POUNDS THINLY SLICED RED CABBAGE

1   CUP THINLY SLICED RED ONION

5   GREEN APPLES, PEELED, CORED, AND THINLY SLICED

¾   CUP SUGAR

1¼   CUPS STE. GENEVIEVE CABERNET SAUVIGNON

¾   CUPS BALSAMIC VINEGAR

  SALT AND BLACK PEPPER TO TASTE

Put all ingredients into pot and simmer for 1½ hours. Adjust seasonings.

Currant Sauce

4   OUNCES STE. GENEVIEVE CABERNET SAUVIGNON

2   OUNCES BRANDY

1½   CUPS DEMI-GLACÉ BEEF STOCK

6   OUNCES RED CURRANT PUREE

  DASH CAYENNE

  SALT AND PEPPER TO TASTE

Flambé brandy and red wine and reduce by half. Add stock and currant puree; simmer for 10 minutes. Strain.

Serve with Messina Hof Private Reserve Cabernet Sauvignon.

Radicchio Game Packets

Serves 6

¼	CUP PEANUT OIL
4	GARLIC CLOVES
1	2" PIECE FRESH GINGER ROOT
4	SCALLIONS, CHOPPED
1	STALK LEMONGRASS, TENDERHEARTS ONLY, MINCED
¼	CUP RED BELL PEPPER, DICED
¼	CUP YELLOW BELL PEPPER, DICED
¼	CUP GREEN BELL PEPPER, DICED
¼	CUP POBLANO PEPPER, DICED
¼	CUP CELERY, DICED
¼	CUP NAPA CABBAGE, DICED
	TOASTED CASHEWS
	MINT SPRIGS
	BEAN SPROUTS
	CILANTRO SPRIGS
	DICED TOMATOES
20	RADICCHIO LEAVES
3	POUNDS GAME MEATS, CHOPPED OR GROUND (VENISON, DUCK, PHEASANT)
3	POUNDS COMBINATION OF QUAIL, SQUAB, CHICKEN OR TURKEY
1	CUP PACKET SAUCE (RECIPE FOLLOWS)

Heat a large sauté pan (preferably nonstick) or a wok over high heat. Add the peanut oil, garlic cloves, ginger, scallions, and lemongrass. Cook for about 5 minutes or until browned. Remove pieces from oil and discard oil. Add peppers, celery, and cabbage; stir fry 2 minutes. Push to edge of wok and add chopped game and cook 5 minutes longer. Add "packet sauce" and stir fry all ingredients. Spoon meat into radicchio cups. Garnish with cashews, mint, bean sprouts, cilantro, and diced tomatoes. Serve with dash of sambal BIGA (hot chili vinegar sauce) and eat like a taco.

Packet Sauce

¼	CUP PURE SESAME OIL
¼	CUP PEANUT OIL
½	CUP MUSHROOM SOY SAUCE
1	CUP RICE WINE VINEGAR
2	TABLESPOONS TAMARIND CONCENTRATE
1	TABLESPOON SAMBAL OLEK
1	CUP SUGAR
2	TABLESPOONS GARLIC, CHOPPED
2	TABLESPOONS SHALLOTS, CHOPPED
2	TABLESPOONS GINGER, CHOPPED
¼	CUP SCALLIONS, DICED
2	TABLESPOONS SESAME SEEDS, TOASTED

Combine all ingredients and mix. Store in a tightly covered container.

Courtesy of Bruce Auden, owner and chef, Restaurant BIGA, San Antonio. Serve with Sister Creek Cabernet Sauvignon or Cabernet Franc.

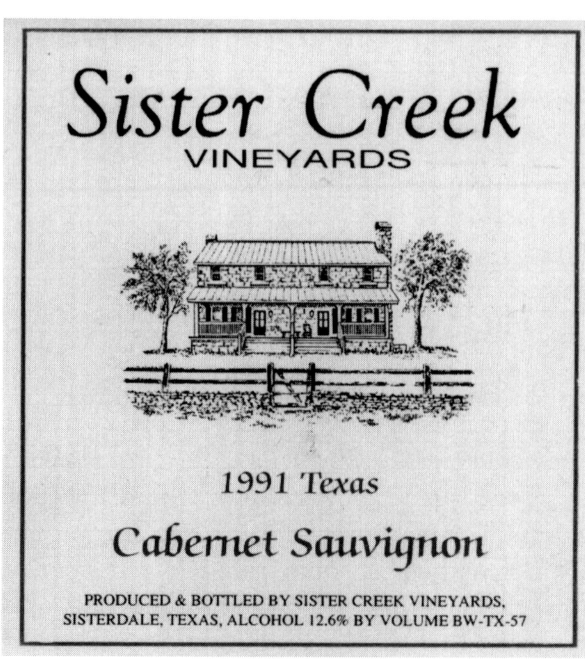

Roast Loin of Wild Boar with Apple Charlotte

Serves 6

1	4–5 POUND LOIN OF BOAR (OR PORK)
1	TABLESPOON SALT
½	TABLESPOON BLACK PEPPER
½	TABLESPOON THYME
½	CUP WATER
3	CUPS GREEN APPLES, PEELED, CORED, AND DICED
½	CUP LEMON RIND
	PINCH OF EACH: GINGER, CINNAMON, CLOVES
2	TABLESPOONS BROWN SUGAR
1	CUP STE. GENEVIEVE SAUVIGNON BLANC
4	OUNCES CALVADOS BRANDY
1	STICK OF BUTTER
3	CUPS OF 1″ CUBED WHITE BREAD
1	CUP APPLESAUCE
	DASH OF SALT
3	EGG YOLKS

Preheat the oven to 450°.

Place the boar in a roasting pan, fat side up. Rub fat with salt, black pepper, and thyme. Add ½ cup water and roast for 30 minutes; reduce the heat to 300°, and roast for another 45 minutes. Remove the loin and keep warm, then skim off some of the fat.

Add the apples, lemon rind, ginger, cinnamon, cloves, sugar, wine, and Calvados.

Return the pan to the oven and bake for another 15 minutes or until the apples are cooked.

Stir in the butter and bread cubes, and roast for a few minutes longer. Mix the applesauce, salt, and egg yolks; pour over the apples. Bake until brown, about 15 minutes.

Place the apples on a heated service platter, arrange sliced wild boar on top, and serve.

❧ *Courtesy of Joe Mannke, owner and chef, Rotisserie for Beef and Bird, Houston.*
Serve with Grape Creek Cabernet Trois.

Roast Nilgai with Agarita Sauce and Herbs, Onion Confit, and Potato and Olive Ragout

Serves 2–4

1   POUND NILGAI (OR VENISON) BACKSTRAP
    (SIMILAR TO BEEF TENDERLOIN)

BLACK PEPPER

OLIVE OIL

SAGE FOR MARINATING OVERNIGHT

To roast nilgai, heat oven to 400°. Brown meat in a heavy skillet, then roast in oven until medium-rare. As there is very little fat in meat, do not overcook.

Agarita Sauce with Sage and Thyme

½   CUP AGARITA JELLY (CURRANT JELLY OPTIONAL)

1   TABLESPOON CIDER VINEGAR

2   CUPS GAME STOCK

2   SPRIGS OF SAGE AND 2 OF THYME, TIED WITH A STRING

½   TEASPOON BLACK PEPPER

To make a stock, brown any bones and meat scraps together with onions, carrots, and celery. Add water to cover and simmer about 6 hours until stock is rich and brown.

In a heavy saucepan combine jelly and vinegar, and cook over medium heat until syrupy. Add stock and reduce by half. If sauce is too thin, mix a little cornstarch with cold stock, and add to sauce while boiling. To flavor sauce, drop in herb sprigs and keep sauce warm until flavors infuse. Season with black pepper and salt. For a creamy rosemary sauce, proceed as above, adding ½ cup of heavy cream when sauce is reduced; then add chopped fresh rosemary.

Onion Confit

1   CUP UNSALTED BUTTER

10   JEWELED ONIONS, SLICED

1   CUP LLANO ESTACADO MERLOT

¾   CUP RED WINE VINEGAR

½   CUP HONEY

1½   TEASPOONS BLACK PEPPER

½   TEASPOON SALT

In a heavy pan, melt butter, add onions and other ingredients. Cook over low heat for about 2 hours.

Potato and Olive Ragout

4   CUPS POTATOES, PEELED AND CUT INTO ½" CUBES

     WATER TO COVER IN POT

2   SLICES BACON, DICED

2   CLOVES GARLIC, CHOPPED

1   CUP TART APPLES, CUT IN ¼" CUBES

¾   CUP CALAMATA OLIVES, PITTED AND HALVED

½   CUP HEAVY CREAM

¼   CUP ITALIAN PARSLEY, CHOPPED

½   CUP BUTTER, ROOM TEMPERATURE

½   CUP ROMANO CHEESE, GRATED

     SALT AND PEPPER

Boil potatoes in water until cooked yet still firm. Strain and reserve the potato and about a cup of the liquid. In a heavy-bottomed pan, cook the bacon over medium heat until tender. Add the boiled potatoes to the cubed apples (some reserved liquid can be added if the potatoes are not cooked enough). Add the heavy cream and reduce until it becomes thick and holds the potatoes and apples together. Lower the heat and stir in the garlic, olives, butter, parsley, and Romano cheese. The ragout should have plenty of body. Season with salt and pepper.

❧ *Courtesy of Bruce Auden, owner and chef, Restaurant BIGA, San Antonio. Serve with Llano Estacado Merlot.*

Sautéed Axis Venison with Port and Orange Sauce

Serves 4

20	OUNCES VENISON LOIN
3	OUNCES CLARIFIED BUTTER
1	CHOPPED SHALLOT
2	OUNCES MESSINA HOF PAPA PAULO PORT
	JUICE OF TWO ORANGES
½	CUP HEAVY CREAM
	SALT AND WHITE PEPPER
	ZEST OF ONE ORANGE
10	WALNUTS
1	OUNCE SUGAR

Cut venison into eight 2½ ounce pieces. Sauté in 2 ounces of clarified butter. Cook until medium-rare. Remove from pan. Add chopped shallot and sauté for one minute. Deglaze and flame with Port, and reduce by one half. Add orange juice and reduce by one third. Add cream and reduce until thick enough to stick to a spoon. Season with salt and white pepper. Pour sauce over venison and garnish with zest of orange and walnuts toasted with the sugar and remaining butter.

Courtesy of Messina Hof Wine Cellars.
Serve with Messina Hof Cabernet Sauvignon.

Venison with Texas Cabernet Sauce and Wild Mushroom Risotto

"This is a recipe I like to use with Texas venison. My family and I are hunters and we enjoy preparing wild game. This recipe is similar to wild game dishes I've enjoyed in northern Italy, where the hunting tradition runs deep. Risotto is a rich accompaniment to the venison; and the meaty taste of the wild mushrooms joins with the roast venison to make a delightful dish to pair with a bold red wine." —Dotty Griffith, The Dallas Morning News Lifestyles Editor and Food Columnist.

Serves 4

2	1–1½ POUND VENISON BACKSTRAPS (SIMILAR TO BEEF TENDERLOIN)
2	CLOVES GARLIC, CUT INTO SLIVERS
1	TABLESPOON PLUS ADDITIONAL OLIVE OIL, DIVIDED USE
2	TABLESPOONS CRACKED BLACK PEPPER
2¼	CUPS VENISON OR BEEF STOCK, DIVIDED USE, RECIPE FOLLOWS
1	CUP MESSINA HOF CABERNET SAUVIGNON
3–4	DRIED WILD MUSHROOMS
4–5	CUPS VEGETABLE OR CHICKEN STOCK
½	CUP CHOPPED ONION
1	CLOVE GARLIC, FINELY CHOPPED
1	CUP ARBORIO (ITALIAN SHORT GRAIN) RICE
⅓	CUP SHREDDED FRESH PARMESAN CHEESE
1–3	TABLESPOONS BUTTER, OPTIONAL, DIVIDED USE
	SALT AND PEPPER TO TASTE
1–2	TEASPOONS ARROWROOT

Rinse and dry venison. Insert slivers of garlic on all sides, using the sharp point of a knife to make evenly spaced incisions. Lightly brush venison with small amount of olive oil. Place 2 tablespoons cracked black pepper on sheet of waxed paper. Roll backstraps in pepper to coat evenly on all sides. Pat in pepper, if needed, so it will adhere. Set aside and allow meat to come to room temperature, about 1 hour.

Meanwhile, combine 2 cups venison or beef stock and wine in a medium saucepan over high heat. Bring liquid to a boil, reduce heat and simmer, uncovered, until liquid is reduced by half. Remove from heat and reserve.

Place wild mushrooms in small microwave-safe dish. Cover with ¼ cup venison or beef stock. Microwave on high 1–2 minutes. Remove and set aside to cool. When cool enough to handle, remove from liquid, reserving liquid, and chop. Reserve chopped mushrooms. Pour mushroom liquid into reduced liquid.

Place vegetable or chicken stock in large saucepan over high heat. Just before liquid boils, reduce heat and keep hot. Meanwhile, heat a small amount of olive oil in large saucepan over medium-high heat. Add onion and cook until onion begins to soften. Add chopped garlic and stir.

When garlic begins to give up its aroma, add rice and chopped mushrooms, stirring to coat with oil and onions. After 2–3 minutes, lower heat to medium and add hot vegetable or chicken stock, about ½ cup at a time.

Stirring constantly, allow liquid to come to a boil. Stir and cook until most of liquid has been absorbed. Continue adding more stock, stirring and cooking until rice reaches the *al dente* stage, similar to the desired degree of doneness for pasta. It should take 20–25 minutes for the rice to cook.

When rice is tender and appears creamy, remove from heat and stir in shredded fresh Parmesan cheese until it melts. Add butter, if desired. Adjust seasoning to taste with salt and pepper. Cover, set aside and keep warm.

Heat a heavy sauté pan over high heat. Lightly coat with non-stick cooking spray. Season backstraps with salt to taste, if desired. Add venison backstraps and cook on all sides until brown. Do not cook past the medium-rare stage (140° on a meat thermometer). If backstraps are large, place at 400° to cook to desired degree of doneness.

Remove from heat and tent with foil to keep warm and allow juices to settle. Pour any pan juices into reduced stock-wine mixture. Heat mixture to boiling and strain if desired. If desired, whisk in 1–2 tablespoons butter and adjust seasoning with salt and pepper.

To thicken, dissolve arrowroot in small amount of water to make a smooth paste. Whisk into strained mixture and cook gently until thickened. Do not allow to boil; keep warm.

Slice backstraps into 1" thick medallions and serve with cooking sauce and risotto.

Venison Stock

1–2	POUNDS VENISON BONES AND TRIMMINGS
1	ONION, QUARTERED
2	CARROTS, CUT IN LARGE CHUNKS
1	SMALL TURNIP, QUARTERED
2-3	CLOVES GARLIC, WHOLE
1½–2	QUARTS WATER

Brown bones and trimmings in a large saucepan or stockpot over high heat. Remove bones and trimmings and reserve. Add onion, carrots, turnip, and garlic. Cook until vegetables are soft and golden. Return bones and trimmings to stockpot and add water. Bring liquid to a boil. Skim to remove foam. Lower heat and simmer until liquid is reduced by half. Remove from heat and cool. Strain to remove vegetables, bones, and trimmings. Refrigerate overnight to congeal any fat. Remove fat. Use in recipes as desired.

❦ *Serve with Messina Hof Cabernet Sauvignon Barrel Reserve.*

Salads, Sauces and Vegetables

Baked Corn and Noodles

Sarah Jane English is a writer, teacher, speaker, travel guide, and media personality who lives in Austin. Her feelings about matching wine and foods couldn't be clearer: "Any wine with a meal is better than dining without wine." Ms. English offers three recipes that are ". . . quick and easy: just add a crisp green salad or savory soup to the Baked Corn and Noodles, Baked Corn and Tamales [immediately following this recipe], *or Grape and Shrimp Salad* [p. 139], *and your meal is complete."*

Serves 6

1¼   CUPS FRESH CORN

2   CUPS COOKED NOODLES

1   CUP WHOLE MILK

2   EGGS, BEATEN

1   TABLESPOON MINCED GREEN PEPPER

2   TABLESPOONS MINCED PARSLEY, SOAKED BRIEFLY IN 3 TEASPOONS SLAUGHTER-LEFTWICH TEXAS CHARDONNAY

   SALT AND PEPPER, TO TASTE

1¾   CUPS GRATED CHEDDAR CHEESE

Combine corn, noodles, milk, beaten eggs, green pepper, parsley, Chardonnay, and salt and pepper.

Spoon into a buttered baking dish and sprinkle the cheese over the top. Bake at 350° for 20 minutes.

Courtesy of Sarah Jane English, author of four books on wine and foods: The Wines of Texas, A Guide and a History; Vin Vignettes, Stories of Famous French Wines; Top Chefs in Texas; *and* Top Chefs in New Orleans.
Serve with Slaughter-Leftwich Texas Chardonnay.

Baked Corn and Tamales

A big fan of Texas white wines, Sarah Jane English says, "Texas grows excellent Chardonnay, Sauvignon Blanc, and Chenin Blanc—a real Cinderella wine that deserves more attention."

Serves 6

10–12	FRESH TAMALES
1	MEDIUM ONION, CHOPPED
1	SMALL GREEN PEPPER, CHOPPED
1	SMALL JAR PIMIENTO, CHOPPED
1	TABLESPOON BUTTER, MELTED
¼	CUP TEXAS CHENIN BLANC
2	CUPS FRESH CORN
	SALT AND PEPPER, TO TASTE
1½	CUPS GRATED CHEDDAR CHEESE

Steam tamales and reserve juice. Lightly sauté onion, pepper, and pimiento in butter, then simmer briefly in 4 tablespoons tamale juice and ¼ cup Texas Chenin Blanc.

Cut tamales into small pieces. Toss vegetable mixture with corn, salt and pepper to taste, and fold in tamale pieces. Put into a 1½ quart casserole and bake at 350° for 1 hour or until the mixture thickens. Remove from oven and top with the grated cheese.

❧ *Courtesy of Sarah Jane English, author of four books on wine and foods:* The Wines of Texas, A Guide and a History; Vin Vignettes, Stories of Famous French Wines; Top Chefs in Texas; *and* Top Chefs in New Orleans. *Serve with your favorite Texas Chenin Blanc.*

Black Bean and Goat Cheese Chimichangas with Avocado Mayonnaise

"The Mexican influence has found permanence in Texas cuisine, and these chimichangas are a nice luncheon dish or an accompaniment to all kinds of fish, poultry, and meat." —Susan Auler, co-owner of Fall Creek Vineyards.

Serves 6

4	CUPS BLACK BEANS, COOKED
2	TABLESPOONS GARLIC CHIVES, FINELY CHOPPED
3	TABLESPOONS CILANTRO, FINELY CHOPPED
½	TEASPOON SALT
½	TEASPOON FRESH GROUND BLACK PEPPER
1 ½	TABLESPOONS POBLANO PEPPER, MINCED
18	FLOUR TORTILLAS
18	TEASPOONS TEXAS GOAT CHEESE (8-10 OUNCES)
	PEANUT OIL, FOR FRYING

In food processor add beans, garlic, cilantro, salt, black pepper, and poblano pepper. Process quickly, leaving some texture to the bean mixture.

Steam the flour tortillas to soften. Place 1 tablespoon bean mixture and 1 teaspoon goat cheese in center of tortilla. Fold sides of tortilla in first, then bottom and top flaps. Secure with toothpick.

Deep fry in peanut oil until golden. Remove toothpicks before serving.

Avocado Sauce

1	RIPE AVOCADO
½	CUP CHICKEN STOCK
¼	TEASPOON SALT
¼	TEASPOON FRESH GROUND PEPPER
2	TEASPOONS SOUR CREAM
	GARLIC CHIVES (FOR GARNISH)

Mash avocado and mix with chicken stock. Season with salt and pepper and add sour cream. Heat slowly in skillet. Pour sauce on each plate and place 2 chimichangas with garlic chives on top of sauce.

❧ *Serve with Fall Creek Vineyards Cabernet Sauvignon, Fall Creek Vineyards Granite Reserve, or Fall Creek Vineyards Semillon-Sauvignon Blanc.*

Broccoli with Pecans

Serves 4–6

4½	TABLESPOONS UNSALTED BUTTER
⅓	CUP CHOPPED PECANS
2½	CUPS LOOSELY PACKED, PEELED AND SHREDDED BROCCOLI STALKS (ABOUT 3 POUNDS BROCCOLI. SAVE THE FLORETS FOR ANOTHER MEAL.)
½	TEASPOON SALT
4	VERY THIN SLICES BLACK FOREST HAM OR PROSCIUTTO

In a small skillet, melt ½ tablespoon butter over low heat. Add the pecans and sauté until lightly browned for 2–3 minutes. Steam the broccoli shreds until just tender, about 3 minutes. Transfer to a bowl and toss with remaining butter and salt. Divide broccoli among four plates. Sprinkle with pecans and arrange a slice of ham on the side.

✤ Courtesy of Hill Country Cellars.
Serve with Hill Country Cellars Merlot.

Cabbage in White Wine

Serves 4

8 TABLESPOONS BUTTER

3 POUNDS GREEN CABBAGE, CORED AND COARSELY CHOPPED

1 CUP MESSINA HOF SAUVIGNON BLANC

1 TEASPOON FRESH TARRAGON

1 TEASPOON CHIVES

1 TEASPOON SALT

FRESHLY GROUND PEPPER

1 POUND VENISON SAUSAGE CUT INTO 2″ SECTIONS

In a heavy 10″–12″ skillet, melt butter over moderate heat. When the foam subsides, add cabbage and sausage, and with a fork, toss it in the melted butter until it is well coated. Add remainder of ingredients. Cook uncovered, stirring occasionally, for about 10 minutes, or until the cabbage is tender. With a slotted spoon, remove the cabbage and sausage from the pan to a heated vegetable dish or platter. Boil the liquid in the pan rapidly, uncovered, for a few minutes to concentrate its flavor before pouring it over the cabbage.

✤ Courtesy of Messina Hof Wine Cellars.

Caponata

Serves 2

1	EGGPLANT
1	TABLESPOON SALT
¼	CUP OLIVE OIL
2	RED PEPPERS (OR 1 RED, 1 GREEN)
2	STICKS CELERY
1	16-OUNCE CAN PEELED TOMATOES
2	TABLESPOONS WINE VINEGAR
1	CLOVE GARLIC
1	CAN (4 OUNCES) SLICED OLIVES
1	TABLESPOON CAPERS

Cut washed eggplant into ½-inch cubes. Sprinkle with salt, mix well, let drain in colander 1 hour, rinse under running water, and pat dry.

Heat oil in large pan; add peeled, roughly chopped onion, diced peppers, and sliced celery. Cook over moderate heat 5 minutes, stirring. Add eggplant and cook another 5 minutes, stirring.

Cut peeled tomatoes into chunks. Add to pan with tomato liquid, vinegar, and crushed garlic. Cook for 2 minutes, stirring.

Add sliced olives and capers, stir well. Simmer uncovered over moderate heat 15 minutes or until most of liquid has evaporated. Season with salt and pepper.

Serve either hot or cold.

Courtesy of Greg Bruni, winemaker, Llano Estacado Wineries.
Serve with any full-bodied red wine, such as Llano Estacado Cabernet Sauvignon or Merlot.

Chunky Chicken Salad

"[Chunky Chicken Salad] is great for picnics, parties and casual dining and is a recipe the whole family is sure to enjoy. Enjoy this festive salad with Fall Creek Vineyards Johannisberg Riesling/ Emerald Riesling, a light sweet wine that compliments this fun chicken meal." —Susan Auler, co-owner, Fall Creek Vineyards.

Yields 1½ to 2 cups

1	TABLESPOON BUTTER
	SALT AND PEPPER, TO TASTE
½	TEASPOON MINCED GARLIC
1	TABLESPOON MINCED SHALLOTS
2	COMPLETE CHICKEN BREASTS (APPROXIMATELY ¾ LB)
2	TABLESPOONS PLAIN YOGURT
2	TABLESPOONS MAYONNAISE
½	CUP FINELY CUBED CARROTS
⅓	CUP SLICED ALMONDS, TOASTED
1	TABLESPOON CILANTRO, MINCED

Sauté chicken breasts on medium heat in butter with salt, pepper, garlic and shallots until done on one side; then flip over and cook until done on other side. Do not over cook, as chicken will be dry. Cool and cut chicken into small chunks. Scrape chicken chunks and pan drippings into bowl. Toss and adjust salt and pepper.

Add yogurt, mayonnaise, carrots, almonds, and cilantro. Blend well and chill. Serve on bed of garden greens or toast rounds.

Eggplant Parmesan

Merrill Bonarrigo, owner of Messina Hof Wine Cellars, describes the following recipe as "an Italian staple when eggplants are in season. The eggplant should be a rich black-purple in color and should be long, slender, and firm to the touch. Select the eggplant with the smallest round demarcation at the end of the vegetable. Large eggplants often have many bitter seeds that detract from their flavor."

Serves 6

2	**MEDIUM EGGPLANTS**
	SALT, FLOUR, PEPPER, AND OLIVE OIL

Peel and slice eggplant ¼″–½″ thick, and lay in single layers on paper towels. Sprinkle each layer with salt and cover with next towel. When all eggplants are cut and stacked, place a plate on top. This helps to extract any bitterness from the eggplant. Dust each slice of eggplant with flour and sprinkle with pepper. Fry in olive oil until golden brown.

Sauce

3	**CUPS TOMATO SAUCE**
¼	**CUP MESSINA HOF CABERNET SAUVIGNON**
2	**TEASPOONS EACH OF SWEET BASIL, OREGANO, SUGAR, GARLIC POWDER**
8	**OUNCES MOZZARELLA CHEESE, THINLY SLICED**
4	**OUNCES PARMESAN, GRATED**

Have casserole dish ready with thin coat of sauce covering the bottom. As eggplant slices are ready, layer in dish. Over each layer of eggplant, ladle sauce to thinly cover. Sprinkle with ½ teaspoon of each: sweet basil, oregano, sugar, and garlic powder. Layer with mozzarella cheese and

Parmesan. Continue layering with eggplant until all is used. Bake approximately 25 minutes at 350°, until cheese melts and bubbles on the side.

❧ *Courtesy of Messina Hof Wine Cellars.*

Garden Greens with Carrot Swirl Dressed with Apples

Susan Auler, co-owner of Fall Creek Vineyards, enjoys making vinegar with leftover wine from the tasting room.

6	TABLESPOONS SAFFLOWER OIL
3	TABLESPOONS TARRAGON VINEGAR
1	LARGE DELICIOUS APPLE, CHOPPED
4	OUNCES SOUR CREAM
¼	TEASPOON SALT
	SALAD GREENS
3	CARROTS, CUT IN A SWIRL WITH ORIENTAL CUTTING BLADES

Combine oil, vinegar, and apple in a pan, and bring to a boil until sugar dissolves. Cool mixture and fold in 4 ounces sour cream and salt. Dress greens with carrot swirls and apple dressing.

Serve with Fall Creek Vineyards Sauvignon Blanc.

Garden Squash with Roasted Peppers

"Squash and peppers grow prolifically in the Fall Creek garden, and this is a delectable accompaniment to almost any fish, poultry, or meat entree." —Susan Auler, co-owner of Fall Creek Vineyards.

Roasted Peppers

Serves 4

| 1 | RED PEPPER |
| 1 | GREEN PEPPER |

Peppers should be grilled or roasted under broiler or on grill until they are charred on all sides. Place in paper bag for 20 minutes, until skins separate from pulp of pepper. Peel skin from peppers and slice peppers into thin strips.

Squash

1 ½   POUNDS YELLOW SQUASH, SLICED

1 ½   CUPS CHICKEN STOCK

1   CUP TEXAS GOAT CHEESE

½   CUP GRATED PARMESAN CHEESE

1   TABLESPOON LEMON JUICE

1   CUP DRY BREAD CRUMBS

1   TEASPOON DIJON MUSTARD

2   EGGS, BEATEN

Put squash in pan without lid and boil in chicken stock until soft and mashable. Mash squash with remaining chicken stock and add rest of ingredients. Bake at 375° for 35–45 minutes in well-buttered loaf pan. Serve portion of squash loaf garnished with slices of red and green peppers.

✤ *Serve with Fall Creek Vineyards Sauvignon Blanc or Chardonnay.*

Grape and Shrimp Salad

Sarah Jane English believes that for today's diets—which emphasize fish, poultry, and low-fat dishes—Texas white wines should be favorites. "They're fresh and delicious and less inclined to overpower the food."

Serves 4

1¼   POUNDS COOKED SHRIMP

1½   CUPS SEEDLESS WHITE GRAPES, HALVED

1¼   CUPS DICED CELERY

½   TEASPOON SALT

½   TEASPOON CRACKED BLACK PEPPER

2   TEASPOONS DRY ST. GENEVIEVE TEXAS SAUVIGNON BLANC OR LEMON JUICE

⅔   CUP MAYONNAISE

1. Combine shrimp, grapes, celery, salt, and pepper.
2. Blend wine or juice into mayonnaise and mix with salad.
3. Serve on tomato or avocado halves and garnish with Boston lettuce leaves.

❧ *Serve with St. Genevive Texas Sauvignon Blanc and hot buttered breads.*

Grilled Squab Salad with Figs, Taleggio, and Pecans

3	SQUAB (PIGEON)
½	CUP OLIVE OIL, DIVIDED
12	CLOVES GARLIC
6	SPRIGS THYME
	KOSHER SALT AND PEPPER, TO INDIVIDUAL TASTE
4	OUNCES SHERRY (OSBORNE)
1	QUART CHICKEN OR VEAL STOCK*
1	SHALLOT, MINCED
3	OUNCES SHERRY VINEGAR
½	PINT FRESH RASPBERRIES
4	HANDFULS FIELD GREENS, MIXED
6	FIGS, HALVED
¼	POUND TALEGGIO (OR BLUE) CHEESE**
¼	CUP ROASTED PECANS, CHOPPED

Preheat oven to 375°.

Partially debone and halve squab. (If serving as an entrée, use one squab per serving; otherwise, half squab per serving.) Remove breast and leg from carcass. Lightly brush bones with 2 tablespoons olive oil, and place in roasting pan in oven. Roast bones until brown, turning occasionally, approximately 45 minutes.

While bones are roasting, place garlic with remaining olive oil in saucepan over medium heat. When oil begins to bubble, reduce heat to low. Lightly fry garlic until brown, 15–20 minutes. Remove from heat and strain. Reserve cloves and allow oil to cool to room temperature.

Place thyme sprigs under skin of each squab half. Lightly salt and pepper squab. Place in gallon Ziploc bag with ¼ cup olive oil and sherry, and allow to marinate 2–3 hours, preferably overnight.

After bones have roasted, place in saucepan with chicken stock. Be sure to add any brown bits from roasting pan to stock. Bring stock to a boil, reduce heat and simmer for 2 hours. Strain through fine mesh strainer and set aside. Place minced shallot in medium saucepan with sherry vinegar, garlic cloves, and raspberries. Reduce until almost dry. Add reserved stock, simmer until ½ cup remains, and strain again. Keep vinaigrette warm if using immediately; otherwise cool and refrigerate.

Prepare the grill.

Remove squab from marinade, drain any excess oil. Place squab skin-side down over medium high coals. Leave enough space between birds, as they have a tendency to flare up while cooking due to their fat content. If the squab do flare up, pull them to the side of the grill until the flames subside. Squab, like duck, should be served medium rare. Allow the squab to cook on the skin side 6–8 minutes, the flesh side 2–3 minutes. Let squab rest a few minutes before slicing.

Place mixed greens (arugula, endive, frisee, lolla rosa, etc.) in a bowl. Whisk remaining garlic oil into warm vinaigrette. Toss greens with half of vinaigrette. Place greens on plate and garnish with fig halves, crumbled Taleggio, and pecans.

To serve squab, remove thyme sprig from under skin, remove thigh from breast, and slice breast on the bias into three segments. Place squab on top of greens, and spoon remaining vinaigrette over the top of each squab.

To prepare ahead:

Debone and marinate the squab, after preparing the sauce and garlic oil a day or two ahead of time. The pecan nuts may also be toasted a day ahead, if held in an air-tight container. The garlic oil is a great thing to have around, as are the fried garlic cloves. (The garlic oil can be increased by increasing the garlic and oil ratios, one to one.) The oil will keep for a few months if covered and refrigerated. The sauce will keep for 5 days if refrigerated and covered.

*Veal stock imparts an added richness.

**Taleggio, originally from Italy, is a soft, surface-ripened, whole milk cheese. The Dallas Mozzarella Co. in Texas produces an excellent American Taleggio. Another blue-style cheese can be substituted if necessary.

❧ *Courtesy of Mark Bliss, chef de cuisine, Restaurant BIGA, San Antonio. Serve with Messina Hof Merlot.*

High Plains Barbecue Sauce

Yields 2 ½ cups

1	CUP LLANO ESTACADO CABERNET SAUVIGNON
½	CUP COOKING OIL
½	CUP RED WINE VINEGAR
1	TABLESPOON WORCESTERSHIRE SAUCE
½	CUP FINELY CHOPPED TEXAS 1015 ONION
1	CLOVE MINCED GARLIC
5	TABLESPOONS SUGAR
½	TEASPOON SALT
½	TEASPOON SEASONED PEPPER
1	TABLESPOON FINE CHOPPED PARSLEY
½	TEASPOON CRUSHED ROSEMARY
¼	TEASPOON CRUMBLED BAY LEAVES
6	WHOLE CLOVES

Combine all ingredients in a jar. Cover tightly and shake well to blend. Store in refrigerator. Shake well before using.

Mary Burge, wife of Stu Burge, Executive Director, Texas Wine and Grape Growers Association, Colleyville.

Hill Country Black Beans

1	POUND DRIED BLACK BEANS
8	CUPS COLD WATER
2	TABLESPOONS VEGETABLE OIL
4	MINCED GARLIC CLOVES
1	MEDIUM WHITE OR YELLOW ONION, CHOPPED
3–4	SEEDED AND DICED JALAPEÑOS
½	CUP HILL COUNTRY CELLARS CHARDONNAY
1	TABLESPOON SUGAR
1	BAY LEAF
1	TEASPOON SALT, IF DESIRED

Wash and sort beans. Place in a large soup pot and add water. Bring to a rolling boil. Remove from heat. Cool one hour. Drain and refill with water.

Saute onion, garlic, and jalapeños in oil. Add the Chardonnay and remaining ingredients to beans. Bring to boil and reduce heat. Simmer until beans are tender (about 1½ hours).

Remove 1 cup beans and mash. Stir back into remaining beans to thicken. Serve over favorite rice, with raw onion, jalapeños and sour cream as garnish.

Courtesy of Hill Country Wine Cellars.

Late Harvest Creamed Peas and Onions

Serves 4

3	TABLESPOONS SOFT BUTTER
2	TABLESPOONS FLOUR
1 ¼	TEASPOONS SEASONED SALT
⅛	TEASPOON DILL SEED
¼	CUP MESSINA HOF CHARDONNAY MUSTARD
¾	CUP LIGHT CREAM
⅓	CUP MESSINA HOF "ANGEL" JOHANNISBERG RIESLING
1	10-OUNCE PACKAGE FROZEN PEAS
2	1-POUND CANS WHOLE ONIONS

Crumbs

3	TABLESPOONS BUTTER
⅛	TEASPOON ROSEMARY OR THYME
¾	CUP STALE BREAD CRUMBS

Blend butter, flour, salt, dill, and mustard until smooth. Heat cream to just below boiling point. Beat in the butter paste. Cook and stir until sauce boils and thickens. Stir in wine, cooking about 5 minutes over low heat.

Pour boiling water over peas and let stand 5 minutes. Drain and reserve liquid. Heat onions in pea liquid until piping hot. Drain.

Combine sauce, peas, and onions. Pour into serving dish and sprinkle with buttery crumbs.

Courtesy of Messina Hof Wine Cellars.

M.D. Anderson Spinach and Red Onion Fritatta

Tim Conley, creator of heart-healthy meals, is a firm believer that wine is a heart-healthy beverage when drunk in moderation. Conley demonstrates his recipes at the annual Fall Creek Vineyards Health Fest.

Serves 10

1	10-OUNCE PACKAGE FROZEN CHOPPED SPINACH, THAWED AND WELL-DRAINED
2½	CUPS NON-FAT COTTAGE CHEESE
8	OUNCES LOW-FAT CREAM CHEESE
1½	CUPS NON-FAT EGG SUBSTITUTE
¼	CUP GRATED ROMANO CHEESE
2	TEASPOON MINCED GARLIC
½	CUP DICED RED ONION
¼	CUP CHOPPED SUN-DRIED TOMATOES
3	TABLESPOONS CHOPPED FRESH BASIL
½	TEASPOON SALT
½	TEASPOON WHITE PEPPER

Preheat oven to 325°. Spray a 12-inch iron skillet with non-stick pan spray. Squeeze all the moisture from spinach. Place cottage cheese in a sieve and press to remove moisture. Combine cottage cheese, cream cheese, spinach, egg substitute, Romano cheese, garlic; blend until smooth. Fold into a bowl and add remaining ingredients. Spoon into the skillet and smooth the top with a spatula. Bake for 1 hour or until firm. Cool for 10 minutes, slice into 10 slices, and serve.

❦ *Serve with Fall Creek Vineyards Chenin Blanc.*

Patate Alla Salsiccia (Potatoes with Spicy Italian Sausage)

Serves 6

7   OUNCES SPICY ITALIAN SAUSAGE

3   TABLESPOONS EXTRA VIRGIN OLIVE OIL

1   ONION CHOPPED

6   LARGE BAKING POTATOES, PEELED AND SLICED

SALT AND FRESHLY GROUND PEPPER

Remove the skin from the sausage and break up the meat. Heat the oil in a large, cast iron skillet. Add the meat, onion, and potatoes, and cook, covered, over low heat for 30 minutes.

Uncover, increase the heat, and saute, stirring constantly, until potatoes are brown. Season with salt and pepper, and serve.

Courtesy of Greg Bruni, winemaker, Llano Estacado.
Serve with Llano Estacado Sauvignon Blanc, Merlot, or Cabernet Franc.

Red River Red Beans

Serves 5 to 8

1	POUND RED BEANS
2	SLICES BACON
1	CLOVE GARLIC
1	LARGE ONION
1	SMALL RED BELL PEPPER
1	TABLESPOON CHILI POWDER
1	CUP LLANO ESTACADO SIGNATURE RED
	SALT AND PEPPER TO TASTE

Rinse beans in a colander. Place them in a large pot with lid, preferably cast iron, and cover with 4 inches of water. Bring to a boil and cook 15 minutes on high heat. Remove from heat and let stand for 2 hours.

Fry bacon until crisp. Drain and dice into small pieces. Return beans to heat and add bacon, crushed garlic, chopped onions, red bell pepper, chili powder, and red wine. Cover and cook on medium heat until beans are tender. Season with salt and pepper, and serve with cornbread or rice and salsa.

❋ *Courtesy of Dr. Roy Renfro, Red River Valley Vineyards, Inc., and T.V. Munson Memorial Vineyard.*
Serve with Llano Estacado Texas Cabernet Sauvignon or Merlot.

Royer's Texas Caviar

30	OUNCES COOKED BLACK-EYED PEAS
½	CUP ONION
½	CUP BELL PEPPERS
½	CLOVE CHOPPED GARLIC
¼	CUP CIDER VINEGAR
¼	CUP MESSINA HOF WHITE ZINFANDEL
¼	CUP SUGAR
½	CUP VEGETABLE OIL
½	TEASPOON SALT
	TABASCO SAUCE TO TASTE

Drain black-eyed peas in a colander; chop onion and bell pepper, and combine all three. Mix remaining ingredients together in a separate bowl, and pour over peas and vegetables. Cover and refrigerate overnight. It will keep in the refrigerator for up to two weeks.

❧ Courtesy of Messina Hof Wine Cellars.

Sauce for Grilling Chicken, Pork Ribs, or Backbone

1	13-OUNCE JAR WOODIE'S COOKING SAUCE
	JUICE OF ONE LEMON
1	TABLESPOON WORCESTERSHIRE SAUCE
1	TEASPOON MEAT TENDERIZER
2	TABLESPOONS MUSTARD
1	TEASPOON GARLIC SALT OR 2 CLOVES CRUSHED GARLIC
1	TEASPOON CELERY SALT
1	TABLESPOON HORSERADISH
	PINEY WOODS COUNTRY WINES HEART OF TEXAS NOBLE RED MUSCADINE

Mix ½ jar cooking sauce and all other ingredients. Fill jar with wine, approximately one-half cup.

Pour into previous mixture. Brush sauce on meat and marinate for about 1 hour. Brush on, while grilling at low heat, to keep meat moist; turn until meat is well done. (I especially like this because it is not as sweet and tomatoey as most pre-mixed sauces.)

❧ *Courtesy of Alfred Flies, Piney Woods Country Wines.*
Serve with Piney Woods Country Wines Heart of Texas Noble Red Muscadine

Smoked Pheasant Salad with Jicama and Texas Goat Cheese

Dressing

Serves 4–6

2   TABLESPOONS MINCED CILANTRO

1   TABLESPOON MINCED THYME LEAVES

1   CLOVE GARLIC, MINCED

2   SHALLOTS, MINCED

1   TABLESPOON FALL CREEK VINEYARDS
      JOHANNISBERG RIESLING

3   TABLESPOONS WHITE WINE VINEGAR

½   CUP OLIVE OIL

¼   CUP VEGETABLE OR CORN OIL
     SALT, TO TASTE

6   OUNCES SMOKED PHEASANT BREAST (RECIPE
      FOLLOWS), THINLY SLICED

4   EARS BABY CORN, BLANCHED AND HALVED LENGTHWISE

½   CUP JULIENNED YELLOW BELL PEPPER

½   CUP JULIENNED RED BELL PEPPER

½   CUP JULIENNED CARROT

½   CUP JULIENNED JICAMA

½   CUP JULIENNED CHAYOTE (A MEXICAN SQUASH
      ALSO KNOWN AS MIRLETON)

½   CUP DICED FRESH MANGO

2   OUNCES TOASTED PINE NUTS (ABOUT ⅓ CUP)

4–6   ROUNDS FRESH GOAT CHEESE, 2 OUNCES EACH

2   TABLESPOONS OLIVE OIL

¼   CUP DRIED CORNBREAD CRUMBS

6   OUNCES MIXED GREENS, RINSED AND DRIED
      (ARUGULA, LAMB'S LETTUCE, OAK LEAF, RADICCHIO)

In a mixing bowl, combine the cilantro, thyme, garlic, and shallots, and mix well. Whisk in the wine and vinegar, and then slowly drizzle in both oils while still whisking. Season with salt and set the dressing aside.

In a separate bowl, toss the sliced pheasant with the baby corn, peppers, carrot, jicama, chayote, mango, and pine nuts. Set aside.

Heat the oven to 350°. Moisten the goat cheese rounds with the olive oil and coat with the corn bread crumbs. Place on a baking sheet and warm in the oven for about 3 minutes while assembling the salad.

In another mixing bowl, combine the lettuces and toss with a quarter of the dressing. Divide the lettuces equally among 4 to 6 chilled plates. Toss the pheasant mixture with the remaining dressing, and arrange the mixture evenly on top of the lettuces. Remove the cheese from the oven and place one round centered at the top of the plate.

Smoked Pheasant

2   PHEASANTS, 2–2½ POUNDS EACH

     ALL-PURPOSE BRINE FOR SMOKING MEATS AND POULTRY

     (RECIPE FOLLOWS)

Arrange the pheasants in a non-metallic container. Pour the brine over, adding water if necessary to cover the pheasants. Weight them with a non-metallic object, such as a heavy glass, to keep submerged. Cover and refrigerate for 12 hours.

Drain the pheasants and pat dry. Let stand at room temperature until dry. Build a fire in a smoker, using the procedure for smoking vegetables. Grease the grill rack and arrange the pheasants, breast side up, on the rack. Cover and smoke for 25 minutes. Turn the pheasants over, cover, and smoke until the breast meat is firm but springs back when touched (about 10 minutes). Serve immediately, or cool completely and refrigerate. Bring to room temperature before using.

All-Purpose Brine for Smoking Meat and Poultry

4	QUARTS (1 GALLON) WATER
1	CUP KOSHER OR SEA SALT
½	CUP DARK BROWN SUGAR
1	BAY LEAF
1	TABLESPOON CHOPPED THYME, OR 1 TEASPOON DRIED THYME
½	TEASPOON BLACK PEPPERCORNS
2	CLOVES
1	CLOVE GARLIC, CRUSHED
1	TEASPOON CAYENNE POWDER

Place all the ingredients in a large stockpot and bring to a boil over medium heat while stirring. Reduce the heat and simmer for 5 minutes. Remove from the heat and let cool. Makes about one gallon.

❧ *Courtesy of Stephan Pyles, owner and chef, Star Canyon Restaurant, Dallas. Serve with Fall Creek Johannisberg Riesling.*

Stuffed Cabbage

Serves 4–5

- 1 LARGE HEAD OF CABBAGE
- 1 TABLESPOON BACON DRIPPINGS OR VEGETABLE OIL
- 1 MEDIUM ONION, CHOPPED
- 1 CLOVE GARLIC, MINCED
- 1 POUND LEAN GROUND BEEF
- SALT AND PEPPER, TO TASTE
- 2 TABLESPOONS PARSLEY
- JUICE OF ½ LEMON
- 1 EGG
- 4 TABLESPOONS BUTTER
- 1 TABLESPOON FLOUR
- 1 8-OUNCE CAN TOMATOES, OR 1 CUP FRESH TOMATOES, PEELED
- ½ CUP TEXAS RED WINE
- 1 CUP SOUR CREAM

Heat water in a pot large enough to hold the head of cabbage. Cover and simmer for 10 minutes. Drain the cabbage and, when cool enough to handle, remove 12 of the largest leaves. The remainder of the cabbage can be used for soup.

In a frying pan, melt the drippings or oil. Gently fry the onions and garlic just until limp. Mix the beef in a bowl with the salt, pepper, parsley, lemon juice, egg, cooked onion, and garlic. Blend well. This will be the stuffing.

Fill each cabbage leaf with a heaping tablespoon of the stuffing. Roll the leaf around the filling, using a toothpick to hold together if necessary.

Melt the butter in a frying pan. Brown the rolls lightly. Carefully place the rolls in a flat baking dish. Blend the flour into the juice remaining in the pan, stirring to make a smooth paste. Add tomatoes, wine, and sour cream. Cook for a minute, to blend. Pour this sauce over the rolls in the baking dish. Cover and bake at 325° for 45 minutes. Hot steamed rice or mashed potatoes will go well with this treat.

Courtesy of Betty Evans, cooking instructor, food editor, and author of ten cookbooks, including America's Regional Cookbook.
Serve with your favorite Texas red wine.

Stir-fried Sautéed Brunch for Two

Serves 2

1	FROZEN HASH BROWN POTATO, THAWED
1	SLICE VIRGINIA BAKED HAM, ABOUT ¼″ × 5″
1	STICK CELERY
½	BELL PEPPER
8	SMALL MUSHROOMS
4	GREEN ONIONS
3	CLOVES GARLIC, PRESSED
1	TEASPOON DILL WEED
1	TABLESPOON PARSLEY FLAKES
½	TEASPOON THYME
½	TEASPOON BLACK PEPPER
½	TEASPOON SALT
¼	CUP PINEY WOODS COUNTRY WINES TEXAS MOON WHITE MUSCADINE

Cut potato patty, ham, and vegetables in pieces as if for salad, about ¾-inch pieces. In a 10″ fry pan coated with non-stick cooking spray, sauté mushrooms over medium-low heat until they begin to brown; then add balance of vegetables, potatoes, and ham, and sprinkle with seasonings. Cover and simmer until vegetables begin to soften, approximately 2–3 minutes. Remove lid, add wine, and continue to stir 2–3 more minutes. Remove from pan and divide onto two breakfast plates. Serve with garlic toast and fresh strawberries or other fresh fruit.

❧ *Courtesy of Alfred Flies, Piney Woods Country Wines.*
Good when served with coffee. Better when served with champagne!

Thai Vegetable Salad Topped with Grilled Salmon

10	OUNCES SESAME GINGER DRESSING (RECIPE FOLLOWS)
4	4-OUNCE SALMON FILLETS MARINATED IN 8 OUNCES SESAME GINGER DRESSING FOR 1 HOUR
1	CUP SHIITAKE MUSHROOMS, JULIENNED
6	CUPS SHREDDED SPINACH
1	CUP CHOPPED ROASTED CASHEWS
½	CUP CHOPPED SHALLOTS
1	CUP RED AND YELLOW BELL PEPPERS, JULIENNED
1	CUP CARROTS, JULIENNED
1	CUP CUCUMBERS, JULIENNED
1	CUP ASPARAGUS (LIGHTLY BLANCHED), JULIENNED
10	PIECES JULIENNED WONTON SKINS, FRIED
	EQUAL AMOUNT OF RICE STIX, FRIED

Either prepare a grill or a heavy skillet over high heat, remove the salmon from the marinade, and cook until barely soft to the touch (about 4 minutes each side). Reserve and keep warm.

Sauté the shiitakes over medium heat with about 2 ounces sesame ginger dressing until barely warmed (approximately 3 minutes). Remove and set aside to cool.

Combine all ingredients except the wonton, rice stix, and salmon in a large bowl, and toss with the dressing. Allow 2 ounces per serving. When ingredients are well coated with dressing, gently toss in wontons and rice stix, as these will only remain crisp for a short period of time. Arrange salad on a large plate and top with grilled salmon.

Sesame Ginger Dressing

4	OUNCES RICE WINE VINEGAR, UNSEASONED
4	OUNCES SUGAR
2	OUNCES SOY SAUCE
1	TABLESPOON CHOPPED GINGER
1	TABLESPOON CHOPPED SHALLOTS
2	TABLESPOONS CHOPPED GARLIC
2	TABLESPOONS CHOPPED SCALLIONS
1	TABLESPOON TOASTED SESAME SEEDS
1	TABLESPOON Sambal Olek OR SIMILAR CHILI SAUCE
	JUICE OF 1 LIME
	SALT AND WHITE PEPPER TO TASTE
2	OUNCES PEANUT OIL
1	OUNCE PURE SESAME OIL

Combine all ingredients except oils in a mixing bowl and whisk together well. Slowly pour in oils while continuing to whisk.

Courtesy of Bruce Auden, owner and chef, Restaurant BIGA, San Antonio. Serve with Fall Creek Sauvignon Blanc.

Veggi Salad

Salad

2	SMALL PORTIONS OF FRESH BABY GREENS	Serves 2 as
6	SLICES BACON, COOKED UNTIL CRISP AND GOLDEN, DRAINED AND ROUGHLY CHOPPED	dinner, or 4
8	OUNCES MEDIUM SHRIMP WITH TAILS—DO NOT OVERCOOK (2 MINUTES TOPS!)	as appetizer
1	POUND GREEN BEANS, 1″ LENGTHS, COOKED LIGHTLY AND DRAINED	
4	MEDIUM ROMA TOMATOES, CUT INTO BITE SIZE PIECES	
1	MEDIUM RED ONION CUT INTO MEDIUM DICE	
2	TABLESPOONS CHOPPED FRESH PARSLEY	
1	8-OUNCE CAN WHITE BEANS (GREAT NORTHERN STYLE), DRAINED AND GENTLY RINSED	

Vinaigrette

Whisk together ¼ cup olive oil, ¼ cup safflower oil, juice and grated zest of 1 lemon, ¼ teaspoon tarragon leaves, cracked black pepper, and garlic salt to taste.

Gently combine and toss all salad ingredients in a large flat bowl. Add vinaigrette and toss to coat well. Sprinkle with cracked pepper to taste.
Divide additional baby greens on salad plates and top with vinaigrette.

*Courtesy of Sylvia and Kim McPherson, winemakers, Cap*Rock Winery. Serve with Cap*Rock Cabernet Royale, Rosé of Cabernet Sauvignon, well chilled.*

Winemaker's Omelet

One of Paul Bonarrigo's favorite activities is to wake up on Sunday mornings and create something in the kitchen. This is one of the Messina Hof winemaker's favorite dishes.

Serves 3

3	ITALIAN SAUSAGES CUT INTO 1″ PIECES
½	TEASPOON PARSLEY
¼	TEASPOON FENNEL
½	TEASPOON THYME
3	EGGS
⅛	CUP FRENCH-STYLE DRESSING
⅛	CUP MESSINA HOF JOHANNISBERG RIESLING
½	TEASPOON GARLIC, MINCED
½	TEASPOON SWEET BASIL
11	OUNCES CREAM CHEESE

Fry sausage with spices. Beat eggs until frothy; add dressing and Johannisberg Riesling. Pour into heated omelet pan. Sprinkle with garlic and basil.

Fill omelet with sausage mixture. Fold omelet when edges are cooked. Top with thinly sliced cream cheese. Cook until cheese melts.

❧ *Courtesy of Messina Hof Wine Cellars.*

Pasta and Breadstuffs

Crab Stuffing

*"Sauvignon Blanc seems to have been created especially for crab. This stuffing recipe has become a staple in our home. We use with dishes such as stuffed crab, stuffed flounder, and stuffed mushroom caps." —*Merrill Bonarrigo, co-owner, Messina Hof Wine Cellars.

1	10-OUNCE CAN RED OR FRESH CRAB MEAT
2	EGGS, BEATEN
1	TEASPOON MESSINA HOF SAUVIGNON BLANC
1	TEASPOON DILL WEED
1	TEASPOON GARLIC POWDER
1	TEASPOON CLOVES, GROUND
1	TEASPOON CILANTRO
	SALT, PEPPER TO TASTE
1	TEASPOON RANCH-STYLE DRESSING
¼	CUP ROMANO CHEESE
¼	CUP BREAD CRUMBS

Mix ingredients together. Use as a stuffing on your favorite dish.

For Fish: Cut pocket in fish and stuff or layer 2 fish fillets with stuffing between. A long fillet can be rolled pinwheel style with stuffing. Brush with butter. Bake 40 minutes at 350°. Baste with butter.

For Mushrooms: Destem mushrooms. Dice stems and include in stuffing. Sauté mushroom caps in butter and stuff. Place on buttered pans, and top with additional cheese. Broil 10 minutes and baste with butter.

Serve with Messina Hof Sauvignon Blanc.

Focaccia Rolls with Arina Goat Cheese, Shiitake Mushrooms and Herbs

Dough

3	TEASPOONS YEAST (1 PACKAGE)
2¾	CUPS WATER
7½	CUPS ALL-PURPOSE FLOUR
2	TABLESPOONS OLIVE OIL
1	TABLESPOON KOSHER OR FINE SEA SALT
	FRESH BLACK PEPPER

Serves 4

Yields 24–36 rolls

Combine yeast and water and allow to bloom, about 10 minutes. Stir in 2½ cups of the flour, oil, and salt. Whisk until smooth. Stir in remaining flour until dough forms. Knead by hand or with a dough hook until smooth and soft, about 6–10 minutes. The dough should be soft and moist, but not sticky. Add extra flour if necessary. Place dough in an oiled bowl and cover with a linen towel. Let rise until doubled, 1½–2½ hours, depending on room temperature.

Filling

1½ POUNDS SHIITAKE MUSHROOMS, JULIENNED

2 TABLESPOONS OLIVE OIL

1 TEASPOON GARLIC, CHOPPED

2 TABLESPOONS THYME

4–6 TABLESPOONS ROSEMARY

12 OUNCES GOAT CHEESE OR OTHER SEMI-HARD CHEESE

OPTIONAL: CHIVES, SAGE

KOSHER SALT AND PEPPER, TO TASTE

OLIVE OIL, FOR DRIZZLING

Sauté mushrooms in oil. When they are half cooked, add garlic. Allow to cool and toss in 1 tablespoon each thyme and rosemary. Set aside mixture. Shave or grate cheese, set aside.

Grease and sprinkle cornmeal on jelly roll pan. Preheat oven to 400°. Turn dough onto lightly floured surface and divide in half. Pat or roll each piece into a 10″ × 15″ rectangle. Spread on mushrooms and cheese and roll up. Slice 2″-thick pieces and place in pan. Cover and allow to rise again until doubled. Sprinkle with herbs, salt, and fresh pepper. Drizzle with oil. Bake at 350° for 20–25 minutes When done, remove from oven and invert on racks so the bottom doesn't become soggy. Serve warm or room temperature. Do not refrigerate.

✤ *Serve with Fall Creek Vineyards Chardonnay.*

Fondue

Serves 6

1   .750 LITER BOTTLE WIMBERLEY VALLEY SAUVIGNON BLANC OR CHENIN BLANC

½   GARLIC CLOVE

1   POUND MILD CHEESE, GRATED (SWISS, EMMENTHALER, HAVARTI, ETC.)

2   TABLESPOONS FLOUR

    PINCH OF NUTMEG

    SALT AND PEPPER, TO TASTE

2   OUNCES KIRSCHWASSER (CHERRY BRANDY)

1   LOAF FRENCH BREAD, 2 DAYS OLD

In fondue pot, bring wine and garlic clove to boil; remove garlic clove. Stir into the boiling wine the grated cheese, which has been dusted with flour; season to taste with nutmeg, salt and pepper. Add Kirschwasser. Cut French bread into 1″ cubes for dipping into fondue. Serve with Wimberley Valley Chenin Blanc or Sauvignon Blanc.

❧ *Courtesy of Holger Lobush, Wimberley Valley Winery.*

Grandma's Turkey Stuffing

"I grew up watching my grandmother make her stuffing, and I treasure the memories of numerous Thanksgiving and Christmas celebrations enjoying the fruits of her labor. It was only natural to continue this tradition and, when I started my own home, share Grandma's recipe with good friends. My first Thanksgiving meal was shared with the Giordano family in Gainesville, Florida, some 30 years ago. They continue the tradition and claim that Grandma's stuffing is the highlight of their Thanksgiving feasts. There were no Texas wines in Florida in 1966, but Messina Hof's Gamay Beaujolais or Ste. Genevieve's Merlot make wonderful accompaniments today."—Janice Napolitano, Human Resources Professional, Orlando, Florida.

Stuffs one 10–12 pound turkey

4–5	POTATOES
	BUTTER
	SALT AND PEPPER, TO TASTE
¼	ONION, CHOPPED
¾	CUP CELERY, CHOPPED
½	POUND GROUND CHUCK
½	POUND BREAKFAST SAUSAGE
1	TEASPOON POULTRY SEASONING

Peel potatoes, boil and mash them with butter. Add salt and pepper to taste. Brown together onion, celery, chuck, and sausage. Cool both mixtures. Combine mashed potatoes and meat mixture, then add poultry seasoning. This recipe will suit to stuff a 10-pound turkey. Roast turkey as usual; its juices will enhance the flavors of the stuffing.

Serve with Messina Hof Gamay Beaujolais or Ste. Genevieve Merlot.

Messina Hof Meatballs with Parmesan Stuffed Pasta

Meatballs

Serves 4

1	POUND GROUND CHUCK
1	POUND GROUND PORK
½	CUP ITALIAN BREAD CRUMBS
1	TEASPOON BASIL
1	TEASPOON OREGANO
1	TEASPOON PARSLEY
1	EGG (LIGHTLY BEATEN)
¼	CUP MESSINA HOF CABERNET SAUVIGNON
¼	TEASPOON NUTMEG
	SALT AND PEPPER

Mix all ingredients together and shape into meatballs. Fry in oil until crispy brown.

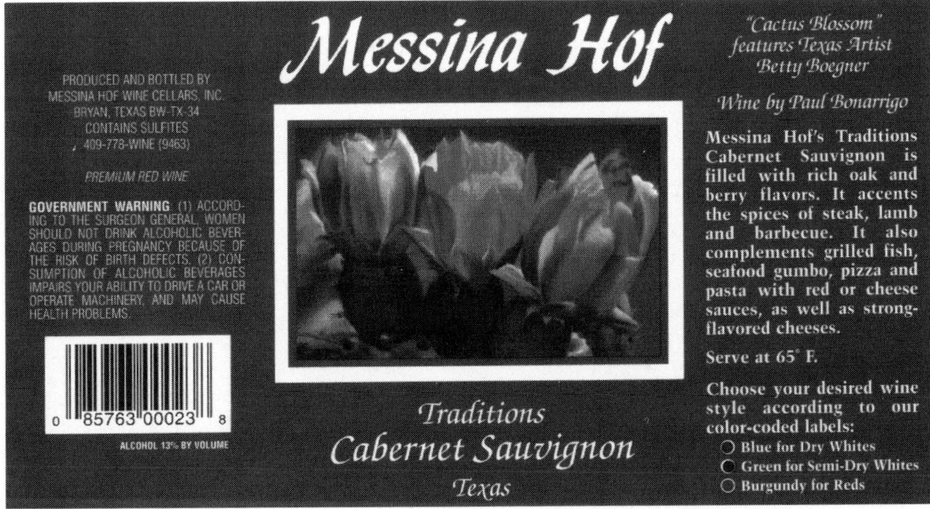

Parmesan Stuffed Pasta

½	QUART CHICKEN BROTH
1	TABLESPOON TOMATO PASTE
2	TABLESPOONS EACH BUTTER AND OLIVE OIL
1	SMALL ONION, SLICED
1¼	POUNDS BONELESS STEWING BEEF
1	STALK CELERY, SLICED
1	CARROT, SLICED
	A PINCH OF CINNAMON
3	CLOVES GARLIC, MINCED
1	CUP Messina Hof Cabernet Sauvignon
6	TABLESPOONS BREAD CRUMBS
9	TABLESPOONS GRATED Parmesan
2	EGGS, WELL BEATEN
	A GRATING OF NUTMEG
2	OUNCES UNSMOKED BACON

First, heat the broth with the tomato paste. Then, in a heavy, round 3-quart enameled or earthenware covered stewing pot, heat the olive oil and butter. Add onion, bacon, and beef, and brown the meat on all sides over low heat for 10 minutes.

Pour in hot broth, which should just cover meat, and add celery, carrot, cinnamon, garlic, and wine. Let simmer until liquid is reduced to a thick gravy (9 hours). Put sauce through a sieve and set meat aside (meat may be eaten as a second course).

Mix the bread crumbs and parmesan into the sauce along with eggs and nutmeg. It should form a thick, stiff paste. If the paste is too soft, add more bread crumbs and parmesan. Use as a filling in pastas.

❧ *Recipe courtesy of Messina Hof Wine Cellars.*
Serve with Messina Hof Cabernet Sauvignon.

Pasta alla Arrabiata

2	TABLESPOONS OLIVE OIL
¼	POUND SALT PORK OR BACON, DICED IN SMALL PIECES
1	CLOVE GARLIC, MINCED
1	ONION, CHOPPED
1	16-OUNCE CAN TOMATOES, OR 2 CUPS FRESH TOMATOES, PEELED
¼	CUP TEXAS RED WINE
	SALT AND PEPPER, TO TASTE
1	TABLESPOON DRY RED PEPPER FLAKES
½	POUND PENNE PASTA
	PARMESAN CHEESE FOR TOPPING

Heat the oil in a large frying pan. Add the salt pork or bacon, garlic, and onion. Stir over medium flame until lightly browned. Add the tomatoes, wine, salt, pepper, and red pepper. Cook, stirring now and then, for 20 minutes. This may be done ahead.

Cook the penne following the package directions. Drain and serve with sauce and cheese on top.

❈ *Courtesy of Betty Evans, cooking instructor, food editor, and author of ten cookbooks, including* America's Regional Cookbook.
Serve with your favorite Texas red wine.

"Pink" Pasta with Shrimp and Scallops

Serves 4

8	JUMBO SHRIMP
8	JUMBO SEA SCALLOPS
4–6	TABLESPOONS BUTTER
½	TEASPOON SALT
3	CUPS LLANO ESTACADO SAUVIGNON BLANC
1–2	TABLESPOONS PINK PEPPERCORNS
3	TABLESPOONS CHOPPED PARSLEY
1–2	TABLESPOONS RED BELL PEPPER, CHOPPED FINE
1	POUND ANGEL HAIR PASTA

Sauté shellfish in a large skillet for 1–2 minutes in ½ of the butter. Sprinkle with salt and add wine. Bring to a boil, then simmer for about 10 minutes. Remove shellfish and keep warm. Add peppercorns, parsley, red bell pepper, and remaining butter to cooking liquid. Reduce liquid over high heat.

Meanwhile, cook angel hair pasta in boiling salted water. Drain pasta, place in large serving bowl, pour on sauce and shellfish, and toss lightly.

❦ Courtesy of John Rydman, Spec's Liquor Stores, Houston.
Serve with Llano Estacado Sauvignon Blanc.

Salsa Salsiccie

- 2 TABLESPOONS OLIVE OIL
- 8 CLOVES GARLIC, HALVED
- 1 POUND SPICY ITALIAN SAUSAGE, SLICED INTO ½″ DISCS
- 1 LARGE YELLOW ONION, CHOPPED
- 3 RED SERRANO PEPPERS, SEEDED AND DICED
- 1 YELLOW BELL PEPPER, SEEDED AND CUT INTO ¼″-THICK SLICES
- 2 14-OUNCE CANS DICED PLUM TOMATOES
- FRESHLY GROUND BLACK PEPPER, TO TASTE
- 1 POUND FUSILLI OR SHELL PASTA

Heat the olive oil in a large skillet. Sauté the garlic over medium heat for 3–5 minutes, until it begins to brown. Remove the garlic and set aside.

Add the sausage to the olive oil, and cook over medium heat until browned. Cover and simmer for 8-10 minutes, until cooked through and no pink remains. Remove the sausage and set aside.

Scrape up any brown bits from the bottom of the skillet. Add the onion, serrano pepper, and yellow bell pepper; sauté over medium-low to medium heat until softened, about 8–10 minutes. Add the tomatoes, reserved garlic, and sausage to the skillet, and bring to a boil. Cover and reduce heat. Simmer for 15-30 minutes until the sauce thickens, stirring regularly. Add pepper to taste.

Fill a large pot of cold water to a rolling boil and add the pasta. Cook just until the pasta begins to soften. Drain and toss the pasta and sauce together in the skillet. Cook for one to two minutes. Top with freshly grated Parmesan cheese and serve.

❀ *Courtesy of Greg Giordano, Houston architect, amateur cook, and author's oldest son.*
Serve with Messina Hof Merlot.

# Susan's Texas Pizza

"This recipe combines several foods dear to Texans' hearts: tortillas, peppers, and goat cheese in a non-traditional pizza. Use a baked flour tortilla as the pizza crust. This dish is easy and quick to make. Grilled meats can be added for a heartier meal item." —Susan Auler, co-owner, Fall Creek Vineyards.

Serves 5 as appetizer, or 2 as dinner

1	9"–10" FLOUR TORTILLA
4	TOMATOES, SKINS REMOVED AND SEEDED
½	TEASPOON SALT
1	TEASPOON FRESH OREGANO, MINCED
4	TEASPOONS FRESH CILANTRO, MINCED
1	TABLESPOON POBLANO CHILE, MINCED
1	TABLESPOON GARLIC, MINCED
2	CUPS EGGPLANT CUBES (CUT INTO ⅜" CUBES)
2	TABLESPOONS UNSALTED BUTTER
6	OUNCES TEXAS GOAT CHEESE
1	AVOCADO

Score tortilla into ten equal wedges with pizza cutter. Do not cut tortilla all the way through. This enables tortilla to be broken easily into wedges prior to serving. Place tortilla in tart pan (with removable bottom) so that edges barely curl up side of pan; bake until brown, approximately 10 minutes at 350°. Purée tomatoes, salt, oregano, and cilantro in food processor. Sauté poblano chile, garlic, and eggplant in butter; add tomato mixture and continue to cook until mixture thickens and moisture evaporates. Crumble goat cheese evenly on toasted tortilla. Spoon hot tomato mixture on top of goat cheese. Garnish with avocado slices or chunks of chopped avocado.

❧ *Serve with Fall Creek Vineyards Chenin Blanc or Granite Reserve.*

Trenette al Pesto (Trenette with Pesto)

Genoese pesto sauce is traditionally made in a marble mortar by pounding the basil leaves and the rest of the ingredients with a wooden pestle. This prevents the basil from turning black with the heat of the pasta (a reaction usually set off by the steel in a cutting knife). Today it can be made in a blender.

Trenette are fine ribbon noodles, which can be made at home with 3 cups flour, two eggs, and sufficient water to make a soft, smooth dough.

Serves 4

1	CUP FRESH BASIL LEAVES, TIGHTLY PACKED
2	TABLESPOONS PINE NUTS
3	GARLIC CLOVES, PEELED
	SALT
3	TABLESPOONS GRATED PECORINO CHEESE
3	TABLESPOONS FRESHLY GRATED PARMESAN CHEESE
½	CUP EXTRA VIRGIN OLIVE OIL
2	MEDIUM BOILING POTATOES
1	POUND GREEN BEANS, TRIMMED
13	OUNCES NOODLES

Wash the basil leaves and dry them well.

Combine pine nuts, garlic, and basil in a blender. Add a little salt, the cheeses, and a small amount of oil, then purée.

Pour in remaining oil and blend for a further second or two. Peel the potatoes and cut into julienne strips.

Bring a large saucepan of water to boil, drop in beans and cook for 5 minutes. Add the potatoes, and after 2 minutes add the noodles. When noodles are cooked *al dente,* about 5 minutes, drain mixture and turn out onto a serving plate.

Toss with the prepared pesto and serve.

Courtesy of Greg Bruni, winemaker, Llano Estacado.
Serve with Llano Estacado Sauvignon Blanc or Llano Estacado Cabernet Sauvignon.

Vegetable Pasta Toss

"While studying Italian at the University of Florence for a semester, I discovered many wonderful and, more importantly, cheap pasta dishes. This one is a quick and easy favorite that a classmate from California shared with me." —Susan Giordano, a Project Manager for Folio Z, a Technology Communications firm in Atlanta, Georgia, and the author's daughter.

1	POUND ROTINI OR GNOCCHI PASTA
3	TABLESPOONS EXTRA, EXTRA VIRGIN OLIVE OIL
1	CLOVE GARLIC, MINCED
½	SMALL RED, HOT PEPPER, MINCED
2–3	DASHES OF SALT AND FRESH GROUND BLACK PEPPER
1½	CUPS ROASTED RED PEPPERS, SLICED IN STRIPS
2	CUPS ARTICHOKE HEARTS IN OIL AND SPICES, CHOPPED, WITH JUICES
¾	CUP SUN-DRIED TOMATOES IN OIL, DRAINED AND CHOPPED
1–2	TABLESPOONS FRESHLY CHOPPED PARSLEY
	FRESH GRATED PARMESAN CHEESE

Serves 4–6

Cook pasta al dente. Heat olive oil, add garlic, hot pepper, and salt and pepper. Brown garlic. Add roasted peppers, artichoke hearts and juices, sun-dried tomatoes, and parsley. Sauté over medium heat for 5–7 minutes. Toss over pasta and lightly sprinkle with Parmesan cheese. Buon Appetito!

❧ *Serve with Messina Hof Gamay Beaujolais.*

WALNUT CREEK CE
VINTAGE
1984
TEXAS PORT
LIMITED BOTTLING
WIMBERLEY VALL
Messina Hof
PRIVATE RESERVE
PHEASANT RIDGE
Special Reserve
Hill Country Cellars
SLAUGHTER LEFTWICH
VINEYARDS
AP ROCK
1994
CABERNET ROYALE
OSÉ OF CABERNET SAUVIGNON
TEXAS
ALC 11% BY VOL
FALL CREEK
VINEYARDS
ELL MOUNTAIN
ESTATE BOTTLED
STE. GENEVIEVE
Grape
VINE
19
TEX
CHAPE

Desserts

Almond Cake with Balsamic Strawberries and Orange Mascarpone

Almond Cake

7	OUNCES ALMOND PASTE
½	CUP BUTTER
¾	CUP SUGAR
4	LARGE EGGS
¼	TEASPOON ALMOND EXTRACT
2	TABLESPOONS GRAND MARNIER
¼	CUP FLOUR
½	TEASPOON BAKING POWDER

In a mixer, cream the almond paste, butter, and sugar. Beat in the eggs, almond extract, and Grand Marnier.

Sift the flour and baking powder together, and blend into batter until smooth. Pour into a buttered and floured 8″ cake pan and bake in a 350° oven for 30–40 minutes. Top with Balsamic Strawberries and Orange Mascarpone.

Balsamic Strawberries

2	PINTS STRAWBERRIES, STEMMED AND HALVED
½	CUP BALSAMIC VINEGAR
4	TABLESPOONS HONEY

Combine all ingredients and refrigerate for one hour before serving.

Orange Mascarpone

6   OUNCES FRESH MASCARPONE CHEESE

1   TABLESPOON GRATED ORANGE PEEL

1   TABLESPOON POWDERED SUGAR

Mix all ingredients and refrigerate one hour before serving.

Serve with Messina Hof "Angel" Late Harvest Johannisberg Riesling. Courtesy of Jimmy Mitchell, Executive Chef, Rainbow Lodge, Houston.

Beauberries Bordeaux

Beauberries Bordeaux is a very old, traditional dessert used by the common as well as the elite French for friendly, informal occasions. It is simple, fast, delicious and a fun way to top off dinner.

"I was shown how to make and enjoy Beauberries Bordeaux by Chef Claude Candessanche, the private chef of Baron Philippe Rothschild at Chateau Mouton Rothschild for many years. On September 9, 1994, at the 11th-century castle of Chateau Lamarque, Chef Claude and his son prepared dinner for a delegation, and I was the fortunate guest of the kitchen. Beauberries Bordeaux was not on the menu for the delegation, but it was the thrill of the meal for the kitchen staff."
—George Ray McEachern.

- 6 SMALL, FULLY RIPE STRAWBERRIES*
- 6 RED RASPBERRIES
- 6 BLACK SEEDLESS GRAPES
- 6 RED CURRANTS
- ¼ CUP SUGAR
- 4 OUNCES TEXAS CABERNET OR MERLOT
- 3 LEAVES MINT

Place the berries in a large flat bowl. Cover the berries with sugar. Pour the wine over the berries and sugar. Top with mint leaves.

Serve immediately at room temperature.

*Note: Any fruit will work when cut into small pieces.

Courtesy of Dr. George Ray McEachern, Extension Horticulturist, Texas A&M University, College Station.

Blueberry Cheese Cake

Crust

2   CUPS GRAHAM CRACKER CRUMBS

½   POUND BUTTER, MELTED

½   CUP SUGAR

Filling

6   EGGS, ROOM TEMPERATURE

2   CUPS SUGAR

2   8-OUNCE PACKAGES CREAM CHEESE, ROOM TEMPERATURE

1   CAN BLUEBERRY PIE FILLING

Mix all ingredients for crust. Lightly pack in the bottom of a 9″ spring-form pan. Set aside.

Beat eggs; add sugar slowly, then blend in cream cheese. Pour over crust. Bake at 375° until lightly browned on top, about 35 minutes. Cool. Pour pie filling over the top of the cake and refrigerate.

Courtesy of Alfred Flies, Piney Woods Country Wines.
Cake recipe Mrs. Fredric King, The Cotton Country Collection.
Serve with Piney Woods Country Wines Blueberry Wine.

Chocolate Pear Tart

Susan Auler is a lover of chocolate, and many of her recipes include chocolate, sometimes predominating and sometimes in the background, as in this recipe. Pears are a favorite fruit of the Auler family and are grown on the family estate.

Tart Crust

1¼   CUPS WONDRA FLOUR

¼   TEASPOON SALT

6   TABLESPOONS COLD UNSALTED BUTTER,
     CUT INTO BITS

2   TABLESPOONS CORN OIL

3   TABLESPOONS ICE WATER

In large bowl, mix flour, and salt; cut in cold butter. Blend in corn oil and ice water, and toss mixture to form ball. Knead dough lightly to distribute fat evenly, and re-form into ball. Dust dough with flour and roll out to fit tart pan. Chill dough in tart pan for one hour or more. Line 8″ or 9″ shell with foil and weight with rice or beans.

Bake 15 minutes at 400°. Remove crust from oven. Remove foil and put pie crust back in oven for 5 more minutes to brown bottom. Remove from oven and cool.

Raspberry Puree

1 ½ CUPS FRESH RASPBERRIES

3 TABLESPOONS MAPLE SYRUP

2 TABLESPOONS SUGAR

Simmer all ingredients until thickened. Pour through fine strainer.

Topping

1 CUP BREAD CRUMBS

½ CUP PINE NUTS

¼ CUP UNSALTED BUTTER (CUT INTO SMALL PIECES)

½ CUP BROWN SUGAR

In processor, combine all ingredients and process until consistency of oatmeal.

Tart Filling

4 OUNCES SEMI-SWEET CHOCOLATE

1 OUNCE UNSALTED BUTTER

4 PEARS

1 LEMON

Melt chocolate and butter together in small skillet. Line bottom of baked tart shell with chocolate mixture. Peel and slice pears; arrange slices in concentric circles on top of chocolate in tart shell. Squeeze juice from lemon evenly over top of pears. Sprinkle topping mixture on top.

Reduce oven to 350° and bake for 30 minutes. Serve warm, topped with raspberry puree.

❈ *Courtesy of Susan Auler, co-owner, Fall Creek Vineyards.*
Serve with Fall Creek Vineyards Johannisberg Riesling.

Cranberry Cream Pie

2	9″ DEEP PIE SHELLS, BAKED
2	CUPS MESSINA HOF JOHANNISBERG RIESLING, DIVIDED
1¼	CUPS SUGAR, DIVIDED
12	OUNCES FRESH OR FROZEN CRANBERRIES
1	TABLESPOON FRESH GRATED ORANGE RIND
4	EGGS
1	PACKAGE UNFLAVORED GELATIN
1	CUP HEAVY CREAM, CHILLED
	EXTRA WHIPPED CREAM FOR GARNISH

In a saucepan, combine 1 cup Johannisberg Riesling with 1 cup sugar. Stirring, bring to a boil. Add cranberries and orange rind, return to a boil. Immediately lower the heat and cook, stirring for about 10 minutes. Stir in eggs one at a time and add gelatin, softened in 1 cup Johannisberg Riesling with ¼ cup sugar.

Add cream and stir until mixture thickens. Pour into pie crusts and refrigerate. Add dollop of whipped cream before serving.

❧ *Courtesy of Messina Hof Wine Cellars.*

Grapefruit and Champagne Sorbet

"Without the whipped cream, serve between courses to clean your palate. With the cream, decorate with fruit and wafers and serve as dessert." —Holger Lobush

Serves 6

8 OUNCES WATER

6 OUNCES SUGAR

JUICE OF 1 GRAPEFRUIT AND 1 LEMON

2 CUPS WIMBERLEY VALLEY BRUT CHAMPAGNE

WHIPPED CREAM

Boil water and sugar. Add juices and champagne, and freeze.

As a between-course sorbet, decorate with mint leaf and grapefruit sections. As a dessert, add whipped cream when almost frozen.

Courtesy of Holger Lobush, Wimberley Valley Vineyards.

Key Lime Delicious

Serves 4

2 CUPS SUGAR

2 TABLESPOONS BUTTER

4 TABLESPOONS FLOUR

JUICE OF 5 KEY LIMES

LIME ZEST

2 CUPS MILK

4 EGG YOLKS

4 EGG WHITES

CREME FRAICHE (RECIPE FOLLOWS)

Cream butter and sugar together. Add flour, lime juice, lime zest, milk and beaten egg yolks. Fold in stiffly beaten egg whites.

Pour the mixture into one large mold or several individual molds. Bake in a water bath at 250° for 1 hour, until the top is firm and the bottom soft. Serve with chilled crème fraiche.

Crème Fraiche

1 PART SOUR CREAM

4 PARTS HEAVY CREAM

Mix together well and pour into a sealable container. Seal and leave in warm area for 8 hours. Refrigerate and store for up to 2 weeks.

*Courtesy of Bruce J. Auden, owner and chef, Restaurant BIGA, San Antonio. Serve with Cap*Rock Brut Champagne.*

Marble Cheesecake

8″–9″ GRAHAM CRUST

3 PACKAGES (8 OUNCES EACH) CREAM CHEESE, SOFTENED

¾ CUP SUGAR

½ CUP SOUR CREAM

2 TEASPOONS VANILLA

3 TABLESPOONS FLOUR

3 EGGS

¼ CUP UNSWEETENED COCOA

¼ CUP SUGAR

1 TABLESPOON VEGETABLE OIL

½ TEASPOON VANILLA

Prepare graham crust; set aside. Combine cream cheese, sugar, sour cream, and vanilla in large mixer bowl; beat on medium speed until smooth. Add flour, 1 tablespoon at a time, blending well. Add eggs, beat well.

Combine cocoa and sugar in a small bowl. Add oil, vanilla, and 1½ cups of the cream cheese mixture; mix until well blended.

Spoon plain and chocolate mixtures alternately into prepared crust, ending with dollops of chocolate on top; gently swirl with knife or spatula for marbled effect. Bake at 450° for 10 minutes; without opening oven door, decrease temperature to 250° and continue to bake 30 minutes. Turn off oven; let cheesecake remain in oven 30 minutes with door closed. Remove from oven; loosen cake from side of pan. Cool completely; chill thoroughly before serving.

*Courtesy of Greg Smith, winemaker, Hill Country Cellars.
Serve with Moyer Texas Star Spumante.*

Ngaire's Pavlova

6	EGG WHITES (ROOM TEMPERATURE)
½	TEASPOON SALT
½	TEASPOON ALMOND ESSENCE
½	TEASPOON VANILLA
2	TEASPOONS WHITE VINEGAR
1¾	CUPS CASTOR SUGAR (12 OUNCES)

Heat oven to 250°. Place waxed paper on a cold oven tray. Beat egg whites to soft foam; add salt, almond, vanilla, and vinegar. Continue beating for a short time until moderately stiff foam is formed. Add ¼ of the sugar and beat for a short time (about 25 beats with a hand beater). Repeat the addition of ¼ more of the sugar and beat as before. When all sugar has been added in this fashion, finish beating until the mixture forms standing peaks, which fold just slightly at the tips when the beater is lifted. Heap onto waxed paper and bake 1½–2 hours. The color when cooked should be a pale fawn, and the texture of the center should resemble marshmallow. If possible, the cake should be left to cool in the oven with door open.

Garnish with whipped cream or fresh fruit (e.g. strawberries, kiwi).

Courtesy of Tim Dodd, Ph.D., Director, Texas Wine Marketing Research Institute, College of Human Sciences, Texas Tech University, Lubbock. Serve with Messina Hof "Angel," Late Harvest Johannisberg Riesling.

Olive Oil Cake with African Blue Basil and Drunken Berries

"This cake has a wonderful texture reminiscent of an angel food cake. It is especially suited to the hot Texas summer because it is so light. The African Blue basil I get from a local grower, Herbal Gems. It has a slightly peppery flavor that works well with the sweetness of the cake." —Melody Wolfertz, Executive Chef, Marty's, Merchants of Fine Foods & Wine, Dallas.

Cake

Serves 12

1	CUP ALMONDS
1	EGG
7	EGG YOLKS
⅔	CUP SUGAR
2	TEASPOONS ORANGE ZEST
2	TEASPOONS LEMON ZEST
8	TABLESPOONS MESSINA HOF "ANGEL" JOHANNISBERG RIESLING LATE HARVEST
1	CUP + 2 TABLESPOONS CAKE FLOUR
2	TABLESPOONS AFRICAN BLUE BASIL OR SWEET BASIL
7	EGG WHITES
1	TEASPOON CREAM OF TARTAR
8	TABLESPOONS SUGAR
8	TABLESPOONS FRUITY OLIVE OIL
¼	TEASPOON SALT

Butter and flour a bundt pan. Sprinkle with the almonds. Set aside. Preheat oven to 325°.

Bring all ingredients to room temperature. Beat the yolks and one egg with ⅔ cup sugar until a ribbon forms. Sift the flour and salt together. Add the zests to yolk mixture, then wine and the flour, scraping the bowl to ensure it's evenly mixed. Chop basil and add to mixture.

In a clean, dry bowl beat whites until foamy. Add tartar and gradually the remaining 8 tablespoons sugar until stiff peaks form. Fold ⅓ of the yolk mixture into the whites, then gently fold all together. Repeat the process with the olive oil, being careful to retain as much air as possible.

Bake 30-40 minutes, cool in the pan.

Drunken Berries

2	PINTS RASPBERRIES
2	PINTS STRAWBERRIES
1	CUP MESSINA HOF "ANGEL,"
	JOHANNISBERG RIESLING LATE HARVEST
¾	CUP SUGAR
1	PINT BLACKBERRIES
1	PINT BLUEBERRIES
1	TEASPOON FRESH LEMON JUICE
	OPTIONAL WHIPPED CREAM

Lightly crush 1 pint each of the raspberries and strawberries with the sugar. Add the wine and lemon juice, and marinate 1 hour or overnight. Toss in the rest of berries and serve over olive oil cake.

❈ *Note: This cake falls when it comes out of the oven, so don't panic.*
*Serve with Cap*Rock Sparkling Wine*

Peach and Raspberry Crostata

2½	CUPS CAKE FLOUR
5	TEASPOONS BUTTER
5	TEASPOONS SHORTENING OR LARD
⅔	CUP GRANULATED SUGAR
3	EGG YOLKS
	GRATED RIND OF ONE LEMON
1¼	CUPS PEACH PRESERVES
¼	CUP RASPBERRIES
1	EGG, BEATEN
	POWDERED SUGAR

Sift flour into large bowl. Blend butter and lard with a pastry cutter or your fingers until consistency of fine cornmeal. Add sugar, egg yolks, and lemon rind; knead into ball, working as little as possible. Wrap dough and refrigerate for at least 1 hour.

Roll ⅔ of the dough between wax paper and line a 9″ quiche pan. Spread the peach preserves and raspberries evenly. Roll the reserved dough and cut into thin strips for a lattice topping.

Brush with beaten egg and bake at 375° for 40 minutes or until the lattice is golden. Allow to cool. Using a sifter, sprinkle powdered sugar over the top.

Courtesy of Greg Smith, winemaker, Hill Country Cellars.
Serve with Moyer Texas Star Spumante.

Poached Fresh Pear
with Sabayon Sauce

		Serves 6
6	LARGE FRESH PEARS, FIRM	
1 ½	QUARTS RED WINE	
1	CUP SUGAR	
6	CLOVES	
2	CINNAMON STICKS	

Peel pears, leaving the stem. Core from the bottom leaving a ¾ inch hole.

Bring the wine, sugar, and seasonings to a boil in a saucepan. Place the pears in the wine and simmer until tender; be careful not to overcook. Set aside and let the pears cool in the wine.

Drain the pears. Spoon Sabayon Sauce into individual serving glasses or bowls and place the pear in the center. Garnish with fresh mint leaves.

Sabayon Sauce

5	EGG YOLKS
1	CUP DRY WHITE WINE
½	CUP SUGAR
	JUICE FROM ONE LEMON

Beat the egg yolks and add the wine and lemon juice in the top of a double boiler over simmering, but not boiling water. Beat with a wire whisk until the mixture becomes light and frothy. Serve warm or cold.

✺ *Courtesy of Joe Mannke, owner and chef, Rotisserie for Beef and Bird, Houston.*
Serve with Messina Hof "Angel" Late Harvest Johannisberg Riesling.

Poached Pear Bread Pudding

4	TABLESPOONS SOFTENED UNSALTED BUTTER
12	SLICES DAY-OLD BREAD, CRUSTS REMOVED
3	CUPS MILK
4	LARGE EGGS, BEATEN
3	EGG YOLKS
1	PEAR, CUBED
	HANDFUL OF RAISINS
½	CUP HILL COUNTRY CELLARS JOHANNISBERG RIESLING
½	CUP SUGAR
½	TEASPOON VANILLA

Butter bread. Combine with milk, sugar, vanilla, and eggs in a bowl. Soak the pear and raisins in wine overnight. Mix the fruit with the bread mixture. Press mixture into buttered 9″ × 5″ bread pan, leaving 1 inch at the top. Add remaining egg liquid slowly until no more is absorbed. Bake in a water bath, halfway up the sides, in the center of a 350° oven for 45 minutes or until set. Cool on wire rack.

Pear Sauce

1	CUP WATER
1	CUP SUGAR
1	TABLESPOON GINGER
¼	CUP HILL COUNTRY CELLARS JOHANNISBERG RIESLING
3	WHOLE PEARS
1	CUP CREAM
½	VANILLA BEAN

Bring water, sugar, ginger, vanilla bean, and Johannisberg Riesling to a boil. Reduce heat and poach pears in simmering liquid from 20–30 minutes, covered.

Insert skewer to test that pears are firm but cooked through. Let cool in liquid. Reserve 1 pear for garnish. Cut other 2 pears into halves and remove seeds; puree in a blender until smooth.

Whip yolks and sugar until creamy. In a small saucepan, scald the cream. Temper the scalded cream into the yolks. Heat over low heat until mixture coats a spoon. Combine with the pear puree and adjust with Johannisberg Riesling.

To serve, spoon pudding onto a plate. Drizzle pear sauce on top and garnish with slices of reserved poached pear.

❧ Courtesy of Hill Country Cellars.

Poached Pears in Port Wine

Serves 6

1½	CUPS WATER
1	CUP SUGAR
	PINCH OF CINNAMON
2	CLOVES
	JUICE OF 1 ORANGE
	PEEL OF 1 ORANGE
6	RIPE PEARS, FIRM, PEELED. CUT OFF BOTTOM SO PEARS STAND UPRIGHT.
1	CUP WIMBERLEY VALLEY PORT

Boil water, sugar, cinnamon, and cloves. Add pears. Simmer in covered pan (do not boil) for 12–15 minutes. Add orange (juice and peel) and 1 cup of Wimberley Valley Port for the last 3–4 minutes.

Serve in glass dish with sauce, pears standing. Decorate with chocolate shavings and nuts.

❧ Courtesy of Holger Lobush, Wimberley Valley Winery.

Poppy Seed Wine Cake

Mrs. Lyndol Hart, wife of the founder of Sanchez Creek Vineyards in Weatherford, served this delightful dessert to my family when we visited the Harts in the early 1980s as I was researching my book, Texas Wines and Wineries. *Many a guest at our table has enjoyed the same dessert, accompanied by a Johannisberg Riesling or a Muscat Canelli.*

1	BOX YELLOW CAKE MIX
4	EGGS
1	CUP OIL
8	OUNCES SOUR CREAM
½	CUP SHERRY
1	PACKAGE INSTANT VANILLA PUDDING
¼	CUP POPPY SEED

Combine ingredients in order listed. Pour into a greased and floured bundt pan or tube pan.

Bake at 325° for 1 hour. Cool. After cake cools, sprinkle with powdered sugar if desired.

Will stay fresh and moist for a week. Freezes well.

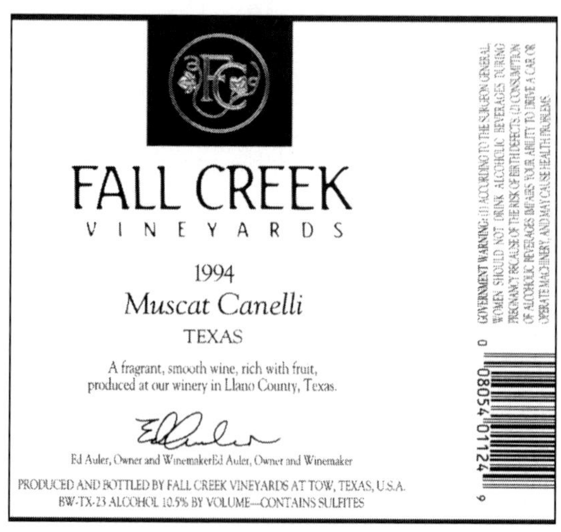

Salzburger Nockerl

3   EGG YOLKS

1   TEASPOON VANILLA

1   TABLESPOON FLOUR

½   TEASPOON GRATED LEMON PEEL

4   EGG WHITES

2   TABLESPOONS SUGAR

    CONFECTIONERS' SUGAR

Preheat the oven to 350°.

Separate the eggs, place the whites in a mixing bowl and the yolks in a medium-size bowl.

Combine the yolks with the vanilla, flour, and lemon peel.

Whisk the egg whites, add the sugar, and continue to beat until whites are nice and stiff.

Fold the egg whites into the yolks.

Generously butter an oval 8″ × 10″ × 2″ glass baking dish. Place mixture in three mounds in the dish, using a rubber spatula.

Bake the nockerl in the middle of the oven for about 10 minutes or until light brown.

Sprinkle with confectioners' sugar and serve immediately.

Either vanilla or fresh raspberry sauce is appropriate to serve with this dessert.

Courtesy of Joe Mannke, owner and chef, Rotisserie for Beef and Bird, Houston. Serve with Messina Hof Gewurztraminer.

Sautéed Pears and Apples

Serves 4

2   RED APPLES

1   GREEN APPLE

2   PEARS

1   LEMON (FOR JUICE AND ZEST)

¼   CUP BUTTER

      GROUND CINNAMON

1   TEASPOON DON TOMAS RUBY PORT (HILL COUNTRY CELLARS)

Core fruit and cut into ½ inch wedges, leaving peel on. Sprinkle with lemon juice.

Melt butter in hot sauté pan and add fruit. Sauté for 3–4 minutes.

Add port and simmer; cook another 3–4 minutes.

Add lemon zest and cinnamon, stirring gently until you reach desired consistency.

Serve hot.

Courtesy of Hill Country Cellars.

Southwest Lemon-lime Tacos with Strawberry Sauce

Tacos

4	EGGS
9	CUPS SUGAR
1	LEMON, ZESTED AND MINCED
¼	CUP FLOUR
9	OUNCES ALMONDS, SLICED

Preheat oven to 375°. Mix the eggs, sugar, and lemon zest. Stir in the flour and then the almonds. On a greased and floured baking sheet, place 1 tablespoon of mixture 4″ apart. With the back of a fork, press the mixture into 3″ circles. Bake until edges are just turning a light brown color. Cool. Bake again until edges are nicely browned. Remove from tray and shape immediately over a dowel to form tacos. Store in an airtight container.

Lemon-lime Curd

3	EGGS
3	EGG YOLKS
2	LEMONS, JUICED
1	LIME, JUICED
3	TABLESPOONS BUTTER

Place the eggs and juices in a stainless-steel bowl and put over a pot of simmering water. Whisk until triple in volume and the foaming action has ceased. Remove from heat and whisk in the butter that has been cut in small pieces. Cool. Then fill tacos halfway.

Meringue

    1   CUP EGG WHITES
    1½   CUPS SUGAR

Heat the egg whites and sugar in a mixing bowl over simmering water while constantly stirring. Remove from heat and whip to stiff peaks. Using a pastry bag fitted with a plain pastry tube, decorate the tacos. Using a propane gas canister on medium heat, carefully brown the meringue.

Strawberry Sauce

    1   QUART STRAWBERRIES
    ½   TABLESPOON LEMON JUICE
    ¼   CUP POWDERED SUGAR

Puree and strain. Spoon over tacos.

Candied Lemon/Lime

    5   OUNCES SUGAR, TWICE
    1   CUP WATER, TWICE
         ZEST OF 3 LEMONS
         ZEST OF 2 LIMES

Slowly simmer the zests in separate pots approximately one hour. Pour over tacos and drizzle on serving dish for decoration.

Garnish

❧ *Courtesy of Randy Gehman, Pastry Chef, Four Seasons Resort and Club, Las Colinas, Dallas.*
Serve with Fall Creek Vineyards Emerald Riesling.

Strawberry Port Wine Sauce

Yields 4 cups

2	PINTS FRESH STRAWBERRIES
½	CUP SUGAR
1	TABLESPOON CORNSTARCH
½	CUP DON LUIS TAWNY PORT

Wash, hull, and halve strawberries. Combine with sugar and stir. Dissolve cornstarch in wine and stir into berry mixture. Cook over medium heat, stirring until sauce thickens and bubbles (about 5 minutes). Cool to room temperature and store in refrigerator. To serve, spoon over vanilla or chocolate ice cream, pound cake, or Salzburger Nockerl.

❧ *Courtesy of Linda Qualia, co-owner of Val Verde Winery, Del Rio.*

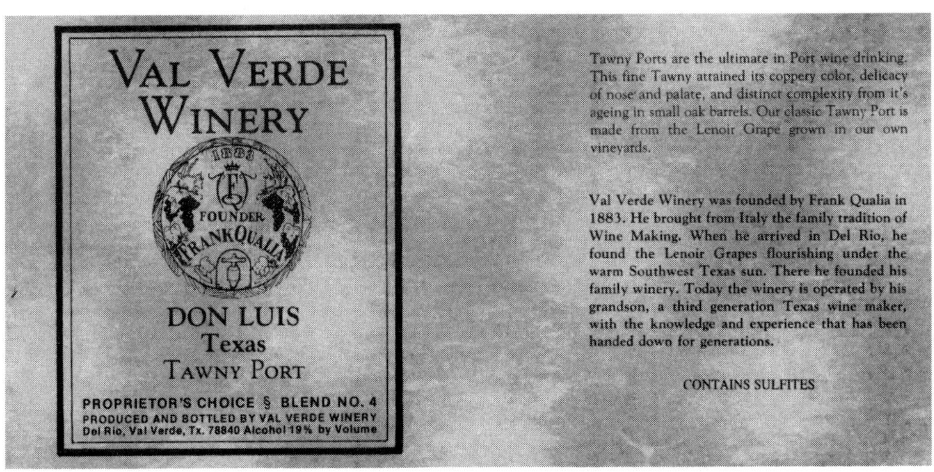

Summer Fruit and Wine Cup

Serves 4

4	CUPS HULLED FRESH STRAWBERRIES OR RASPBERRIES
½	CUP MESSINA HOF JOHANNISBERG RIESLING
1	CUP PLAIN YOGURT
2	CUPS ICE WATER (FOR THICKNESS)
½	CUP SUGAR (FOR SWEETNESS)

Whirl berries in a blender with Johannisberg Riesling. Strain to remove seeds, if you so desire. Return to the blender with yogurt, water, and sugar. Taste and adjust water and sugar for consistency and sweetness. Chill for at least 1 hour. Spoon into 4 serving cups.

*❧ Courtesy of Messina Hof Wine Cellars.
Serve with Messina Hof Johannisberg Riesling.*

Texas Best Cheesecake

Crust

Serves
10–12

40	VANILLA WAFERS
6	OUNCES MARGARINE
½	CUP CONFECTIONERS' SUGAR
1	TEASPOON CINNAMON

Crumble cookies to fine powder. Melt margarine and add to cookies along with sugar and cinnamon. Press mixture into 9″ springform pan. Bake 10 minutes in 350° oven. Remove from heat and cool while preparing filling.

Filling

24	OUNCES CREAM CHEESE
1	CUP GRANULATED SUGAR
4	EGGS
1½	TEASPOONS VANILLA
1	TEASPOON GRATED LEMON ZEST
1½	CUPS SOUR CREAM

Cream the cheese and sugar until smooth. Add eggs one at a time, beating well after each addition. Add vanilla, lemon zest, and sour cream, blending thoroughly. Pour into crust and bake at 375° at least 40 minutes. Cooking time may vary depending on your oven. Look for light brown top and a partially set center. Cracking on the surface of the cake can be reduced by placing a pan of water on the rack below the cheesecake during baking. Refrigerate at least five hours. (Best to bake the day before serving.)

Topping

1	10-OUNCE PACKAGE FROZEN BLACK CHERRIES
¾	CUP GRANULATED SUGAR
1–2	TEASPOONS CORN STARCH

Defrost cherries and pour juice into saucepan. Bring to low boil, stirring constantly. Add sugar. Remove a couple of tablespoons of juice to a separate bowl and stir in cornstarch until dissolved. Return mixture to saucepan and add cherries. Cook until desired consistency is reached (mixture will thicken as it cools). Place cooled topping on chilled cheesecake and serve.

❧ *Serve with Ste. Genevieve Cabernet Sauvignon.*
Courtesy of Don Brady, winemaker, Ste. Genevieve Winery.

Texmati Rice Pudding

Serves 12

1   PINT HALF AND HALF

1   PINT HEAVY CREAM

½   CUP TEXMATI RICE

½   CUP SUGAR

1   DROP ALMOND EXTRACT

¼   VANILLA BEAN, SPLIT

     PINCH SALT

2   EGG YOLKS

½   PINT HEAVY CREAM, WHIPPED

Combine first seven ingredients in a heavy pan, bring to a boil, and reduce heat to simmer for 1 hour or until mixture becomes thick. Stir often to prevent sticking.

Remove pan from heat and take out vanilla bean. Briskly stir in yolks while mixture is hot.

Cool mixture in refrigerator.

When completely cooled, fold in whipped cream.

Serve with raspberry or other fruit preserve.

Courtesy of Bruce J. Auden, owner and chef, Restaurant BIGA, San Antonio. Serve with Messina Hof "Angel" Johannisberg Riesling.

Toasted Pecan Pie with Orange Sauce

"The pecan is indigenous to Texas and is a favorite of all Texans. When the pecan is toasted, it acquires a richer flavor and yet the fat is reduced." —Susan Auler, co-owner of Fall Creek Vineyards.

Tart Crust

1¼   CUP CAKE FLOUR

¼   TEASPOON SALT

6   TABLESPOONS COLD UNSALTED BUTTER, CUT INTO BITS

2   TABLESPOONS CORN OIL

3   TABLESPOONS ICE WATER

In large bowl, mix flour and salt and cut in cold butter; blend in corn oil and ice water and toss mixture to form ball. Knead dough lightly to distribute fat evenly and reform into ball. Dust dough with flour and roll out to fit 8″ or 9″ tart pan. Chill dough in tart pan for 1 hour or more. Line shell with foil and weight with rice or beans. Bake 15 minutes at 400°. Remove crust from oven and reduce heat to 375°. Remove foil and put pie crust back in oven for 5 more minutes to brown bottom of crust. Remove from oven and set aside.

Pie Filling

½   CUP DARK BROWN SUGAR

2   TABLESPOONS FLOUR

½   TEASPOON SALT

2   TABLESPOONS MELTED BUTTER

8   OUNCES SOUR CREAM

½   CUP WHITE CORN SYRUP

¼   CUP MAPLE SYRUP

1   TEASPOON VANILLA

4   EGGS

1½   CUPS TOASTED PECAN PIECES

1   CUP TOASTED PECAN HALVES

In large bowl, mix brown sugar, flour, and salt. Add butter, sour cream, both syrups, vanilla, and eggs. Mix well. Fold in pecan pieces and pour into partially baked pie shell. Place pecan halves in concentric circles on top. Bake 25–30 minutes until filling is set.

Orange Sauce

Yields 3 cups

1   CUP SUGAR

2   TABLESPOONS CORNSTARCH

¼   TEASPOON SALT

2   CUPS BOILING WATER

2   TABLESPOONS BUTTER

2   TABLESPOONS GRATED ORANGE RIND

6   TABLESPOONS FRESH ORANGE JUICE

2   TABLESPOONS FRESH LEMON JUICE

1   TABLESPOON GRAND MARNIER

Mix sugar, cornstarch, and salt, and gradually stir in boiling water. Cook over low heat until thickened and clear, stirring constantly. Remove sauce from heat and stir in butter, orange rind, orange juice, Grand Marnier and lemon juice. Serve with pecan pie.

❧ *Serve with Fall Creek Vineyards Sweet Johannisberg Riesling or Fall Creek Vineyards Muscat Canelli.*

Index

A

B

N

O

P

T